Commands of Christ

Sep

Commands of Christ

Paul S. Minear

Abingdon Press
Nashville—New York

COMMANDS OF CHRIST

Library of Congress Cataloging in Publication Data

MINEAR, PAUL SEVIER, 1906- Commands of Christ. Includes bibliographical references. 1. Jesus Christ—Teachings. I. Title.
BS2415.M53 232.9'54 72-2926

ISBN 0-687-09113-6

MANUFACTURED BY THE PARTHENON PRESS AT
NASHVILLE, TENNESSEE, UNITED STATES OF AMERICA

To my colleagues

Charles Moeller
Theodore M. Hesburgh, C.S.C.

Contents

1 Jesus and Modern Man

The Imperative mood is the very warp on which that sacred pattern of humanity is woven: tamper with those strong Imperative threads and the whole web must ravel.

Richard Hughes,
The Fox in the Attic

This study has a single aim: a better understanding of the commands of Christ. Though single, the aim is by no means simple. Because the commands reach us through the medium of literary documents, a better understanding of the commands requires a clearer knowledge of that medium. Since the force of each command depends upon its context in particular human situations, and since that context changed often during the development of the New Testament, we must seek to trace those changes. To achieve this objective, therefore, I have of necessity adopted a complex method. I shall select a dozen representative commands, trace the use of each command by early Christian teachers as they sought to cope with successive crises in the life of their community, and assess the implications of each command for clues to the basic vocation of Jesus and to the ethical stance of his apostles.

Though the goal is clear, the road is lined with pitfalls. Some of these inhere in the character of the materials and in the nature of the evidence. Others inhere in the stance of the modern student. I call attention to four obstacles of the latter sort, two of which are features of the prevailing climate of public sentiment and two are facets in current biblical scholarship.

Aesthetic Admiration

The first feature of the contemporary climate of opinion is the virtually unanimous respect with which men speak of Jesus. Never has he had a better press or fewer avowed enemies. Everywhere he is venerated as a wise man or hailed as a hero. He has become almost immune to criticism, even by men of other religions. So universally do men celebrate his greatness that there is nothing distinctive or perilous in praising him. Even when it was fashionable to shout about the death of God it was also the fashion to acclaim the life of Christ. Time was when antagonists of Jesus delighted in badgering his protagonists. Now, the only conflict proceeds among groups of protagonists, arguing how best to honor him. In this conflict no one wishes to appear in public as his detractor.

It is this very climate which constitutes a major obstacle to understanding Christ's commands. He did not ask for homage but for obedience. He has always had much more to lose from his friends than from his enemies. Admiration has always blunted his sword. It serves to dull the original outrage (*skandalon*) of his mission. Veneration assumes that we know what kind of man he really was and that we approve his demands. It blinds us to their radicalism and inoculates us against being wounded by them. In fact, our well-speaking makes him vulnerable to his own curse: "Woe to you, when all men speak well of you, for so their fathers did to the false prophets" (Luke 6:26).

Not only does our reverence deceive us about the kind of man he was; it falsifies our knowledge concerning the kind of men we are. Our praise places us also under his curse:

Woe to you, . . .
you build the tombs of the prophets
and adorn the monuments of the righteous, saying,
"If we had lived in the days of our fathers,
we would not have taken part with them in shedding the blood of the prophets."

Thus you witness against yourselves,
that you are sons of those who murdered the prophets.
(*Matt. 23:29-31.*)

It is surely true that each speech in praise of a biblical prophet boomerangs as praise of the praiser. It is one of the subtlest forms of self-commendation—subtle and therefore effective. To be sure, we usually read the attack just quoted without a twinge of guilt because of the apparent target: scribes, Pharisees, hypocrites. In this woe Jesus was attacking someone else. But that is a cheap evasion. Jesus was most concerned about hypocrisy among his own followers (Matt. 7:15). The woe cited above was part of a speech addressed to the crowds and the disciples (Matt. 23:1), groups which corresponded to the laymen and the teachers in Matthew's own churches. The greater the prophet, the more worthy of praise, the more dangerous the praise. If it is true that Jesus has never had a better press than today, it is also true that rarely has there been less knowledge of his commands and less inclination to obey them. Recognition of his greatness has served as a substitute for reckoning the costs of discipleship. High time that disciples declared a moratorium on praise and an open season on a more honest study of what his demands require.

In all seriousness the question must be asked about how to explain so total a reversal in Jesus' status. What has happened that a man so universally feared and hated in one epoch should become so universally admired in another? Have men changed? Has Jesus changed? Did his original opponents misconstrue his message? Do his modern friends understand it better? Whatever the explanation, the analyst should hold the teachings accountable, at least in part. As they come to us through the lens of the gospel, many of his sayings are so vague as to invite distortion. Their basic meaning has become so blurred that they can easily be twisted out of shape. The sentimentality of well-meaning but indolent piety has deflected their original thrust. Though society be fragmented into a thousand strident minorities battling for their rights, each minority has been able to claim Jesus as partisan. All this says something about the character of his commands. For example, there is the initial imperative "Repent." That imperative is capable of a thousand definitions. Seldom does the literary context show clearly what specific actions are integral to repentance. Each reader is left free to adopt that definition, that action, which supports his own inclination and habit. This is typical of what happens to many sayings. The moment a demand of Jesus becomes a vague generalization it becomes vulnerable to the distortions produced by pious sentimentality. It ceases to explain the cross and begins to explain the modern popularity of Jesus. At the name of Jesus the modern man bows before these agreeable generalizations (e.g., love, peace, brotherhood) and forgets the denunciations (e.g., "How are you to escape being sentenced to hell?" Matt. 23:33). He prefers the general principles to the specific commands; among the commands, he ignores those which ruggedly resist modernization, and he sentimentalizes the others.

Allergies to Authority

"Commands" . . . . That very word illustrates a second feature of the contemporary climate. Our instinctive reaction to the word indicates a pervasive resistance to all authority. The very notion of obeying a command raises hackles. Significant of this mood is the tendency to avoid such words as commands or demands in favor of the gentler terms principles or teachings. The latter are less imperious and impertinent. They do not assert so absolute a claim. Today it is assumed on all sides that freedom is a supreme value and that assertions of authority destroy such freedom. If theologians, on increasingly rare occasions, talk of God, it is God's freedom that they expound; when as an almost compulsive exercise they talk of man, it is again of his freedom that they speak. Preachers, to be sure, are still fond of repeating the line in the Gospels about the public reaction to Jesus, "he spoke as one having authority." But this again is an expression of admiration, not of obedience. If one were to measure, as he should, the degree of authority by the actualities of obedience, the falsity of the applause would become all too apparent. It is common to speak of Jesus as the great liberator. He may indeed liberate men, but not without their total acceptance of his authority through obedience to his commands. Such a mode of liberation gives a unique definition to the kind of freedom enjoyed by his slaves.

Modern man has ample reason, of course, to distrust appeals to the authority of Christ, since those appeals in our day come to us as the voice of a religious institution. This fact fuses the authority of Christ into the authority of the church. If there is anything on which contemporary men are agreed it is in rejecting the latter. The good press enjoyed by Jesus is matched by the bad press of the church. In almost every protest demonstration the banners could well read "Jesus—Yes. The Church—No." The authority of Jesus can be accepted when it is divorced from the authority of the church, but not otherwise. Sentimental individualists can declare such a separation at will, but one may doubt whether such a declaration is made on the authority of Jesus. More frequently a revolutionary will attribute to Jesus the commands he accepts, and attribute to the church the commands he rejects. In so dividing the commands, he is really marching to the drum of a rebellion that is itself becoming institutionalized. The authority of institutions is not easily evaded, nor can the authority of Jesus be wholly divorced from the authority of the church. The only communal channel through which his commands are mediated is the church. Yet contemporary men readily assume that of all institutions the church is the most archaic, the least flexible, the most arbitrary, the least responsive to personal needs and contingencies. Given the prevailing mood, therefore, treating Christ's authority as a live option is to activate multiple allergies to the institutionalized authority of the church. It is those allergies which tend to condition many responses to the commands of Christ.

Such allergies operate even more subtly and more effectively when we realize that Jesus' commands are formulated in the words of a book. It does not require much insight to realize that reverence for books has reached a very low ebb. Sentences that are frozen into print are regarded as automatically losing their vitality. What is written becomes impersonal, traditional, legalistic. The premium on being up to date is so high that anything found in an ancient writing is assumed to have become irrelevant. So the authority of Christ is confused with the authority of the book in which his commands are preserved; that book, in turn, is seen as the tool used by a religious institution to enhance its own power. How difficult it is, therefore, for a modern reader, responding to a demand of Jesus, to know in what degree he is dealing with Jesus himself, or with an ancient literary document, or with a modern religious institution concerned, as are all institutions, with its own survival. In such a situation a person who wishes to evade a particular command can find plausible grounds for such evasion, while a person who ostensibly obeys that command may in fact be illustrating a quite thoughtless captivity to the legalisms and literalisms of an archaic institution.

Not that the act of obeying a mandate is the best index to the recognition of authority. There are other, more important indices. But it is characteristic of today's mood that the crisis of authority should be defined in terms of obedience—whether an inferior obeys the dictates of a superior, whether in the contest between two wills one proves stronger than the other. We are inclined to conceive authority simply as the power to command and the right to be obeyed. When, as in this book, attention is focused upon explicit imperatives, this conception of authority tends to become dominant. And yet there is a different conception of authority which is even more basic and determinative. Authority embraces (a) a knowledge of reality hidden from others, (b) a correlative capacity to communicate that knowledge, and (c) a correlative right to be trusted. Today's authentic crisis of authority is located here. Who has this knowledge, this capacity, this right? In the Bible it is assumed that the authority of a prophet to issue commands is uniquely dependent upon his knowledge of God, his gift for disclosing that knowledge, and his right to be trusted by the people whom God addresses. The cogency of his demands stems from the credibility of his knowledge of God and the disclosure of his purpose for his people. Those who repudiate the demands deny that credibility; those who trust the disclosure must embody that trust in obedience to the demands. Those who do not obey do not believe. The authority of a specific demand rests not alone in the document in which it is written, not alone in the church which accepts that document as Scripture, and not even in Jesus as the prophetic spokesman, but ultimately in God as author and source. The ultimate issue is the veracity of the understanding of God communicated by his prophetic spokesman. What makes contemporary discussion of Christ's commands so problematic is the tacit denial of the reality of God and of the commission of Jesus to reveal him. So long as this theological anemia persists there will be little comprehension of the ontological significance of those commands.

So much for two features of the climate of public opinion. I want now to mention two facets of recent biblical scholarship which affect readers' responses to the Gospel records.

Scholarly Skepticism

To locate the first of these, let us assume that a modern reader has seriously and successfully worked his way through the maze of such contemporary attitudes as those just described. He has avoided the perversions attendant upon aesthetic admiration of Jesus. He has given priority to the work of Jesus the revealer as the basis of his work as commander. He has distinguished the authority of Jesus from that of Book and Church, without denigrating the latter as medium of the former. He is able to read and to respond to the commands in the Gospels with relative immunity to the obsessions and confusions of public attitudes. But then he has the quite natural desire to consult current scholarly treatments of the Gospels. Here he finds among the reputable writers explicit assertions that few of the commands in the Gospels can be assigned to Jesus with any degree of confidence. He can, of course, reject such a judgment, though he will find difficulty in justifying that rejection on the basis of his own scholarly qualifications. If he accepts the scholars' judgment, what happens to his desire to obey the mandates of Christ? Does it still make sense to ask potential church members whether they will follow Christ as Lord? What does obeying Jesus mean if we have no access to a reliable version of his requirements? What mean the doctrines of incarnation or atonement or redemption, if there is no dependable knowledge of Jesus' own message?

Professor Norman E. Perrin in his book *Rediscovering the Teaching of Jesus*[1] asserts that "the nature of the synoptic tradition is such that the burden of proof will be upon the claim to authenticity." This means that no saying attributed to Jesus can be accepted as such unless and until one can prove that it "comes neither from the Church nor from ancient Judaism."[2] This is the only way to attain "reasonable certainty" that we are dealing with the historical Jesus. By applying such a criterion rigorously, the net deposit of "authentic" material becomes small indeed. The historian's agnosticism is frequently accompanied by a denial of the desirability of greater certainty.

> It is no longer self-evident that the historical Jesus is, in fact, the central concern of Christian faith, and it may no longer be assumed that the major aspect of that faith is to follow the dictates, encouragements and challenges of the teachings of that Jesus.[3]

Put more bluntly, I believe that Perrin is saying that neither is it possible to recover Christ's commands nor, were it possible, would the believer be obliged to obey them. Moreover I believe that he is speaking here for the great majority of biblical scholars.[4] This attitude has so permeated the outlook of sophisticated intellectuals as to dominate their reading of the Gospels and their response to each specific com-

[1] Norman E. Perrin, *Rediscovering the Teaching of Jesus* (New York: Harper & Row, 1967).

[2] *Ibid.*, p. 39.

[3] *Ibid.*, p. 208.

[4] A judicious critique of Perrin's position may be found in M. D. Hooker, "Christology and Methodology," *New Testament Studies* 17 (1971): 480-87.

mand of Christ. When the reader contemplates any command in the Gospel he is encouraged by the specialists to say to himself: "I cannot be sure that this comes from Jesus. Even if it should, the command is no longer of central concern to me as a Christian." It would be easier to allay this suspicion if the challenge came from enemies of the faith. It comes, however, from professional exponents who have on their side the technical tools of scholarship and often the added prestige of ordained ministers of the church. To their conclusions the only open challenge seems to come from simple evangelists of limited intellectual powers who are ill-equipped to spar with scholars. After a century of successes by scholars in their fencing with simple believers, it is easy to suppose that here again victory is bound to go to the skeptics. This supposition saps the strength of many who would otherwise be inclined to take seriously the demands of Christ as recorded in the Gospels.

However, the historical skepticism of these scholars has probably been exaggerated. In the polemical situation in which radical scholars aim their arguments against fundamentalist literalists, old-style liberals, or creedal dogmatists, they are bound to develop their own extreme dogmatisms (e.g., the two conclusions of N. Perrin outlined above). Where this struggle abates, they are often quite ready to admit both that certain accents of Jesus' message can be reliably recovered and that these accents are of substantial importance. Such admissions are frequently offered as concessions, and their significance is minimized. For example, Perrin concedes that the command to love enemies can be dependably traced to Jesus, and yet he hastily passes on to give more attention to traditions not so reliable. In *Jesus and the Word,* R. Bultmann confidently identifies as authentic various aspects of Jesus' message, yet he insists that the work of Jesus is nothing more than the presupposition of New Testament theology.[5] These concessions suggest that the primary concern of Perrin,

[5] Rudolf Bultmann, *Theology of the New Testament,* 2 vols., trans. Kendrick Grobel (New York: Charles Scribner's Sons, 1951, 1955), I, Chap. 1.

Bultmann, *et al.,* is not so much to deny to Jesus the responsibility for many commands in the Gospel as to destroy theological positions which they consider dubious and faulty.

Cultural Changes

An axiom in this theological debate provides a fourth obstacle to genuine understanding of the commands of Christ. This obstacle can be examined more clearly if we assume that the best scholars, having used their sharpest tools, have reached the conclusion that a significant number of the Gospel teachings can be confidently attributed to Jesus. Such and such commands come to us across the centuries from the Galilean carpenter, representing unique elements in his prophetic appeal to his Jewish neighbors and embodying distinctive standards which were embodied in later Christian teaching. Here they are—two, four, ten, or more basic demands which cohered in his central message. What are we to do with them? Presumably Jesus made such demands with the expectation that his followers would accept and obey them. In fact, a man became a follower only by following. But does the same hold for twentieth-century followers? Presumably it would—if the conditions of their lives had not substantially changed. But, as a matter of fact, the situation has changed radically. First-century Galilee—twentieth-century America! The real question is whether anything has remained unchanged between those two times and places. Obviously there is little similarity in food or clothing or marriage customs or forms of worship. The daily problems faced by the citizens of New York appear wholly different from those of Capernaum. What is there in common between modern technology and ancient carpentry, between a 747 pilot and a Tiberias fisherman? Moreover, these contrasts affect more than externals. The meaning of all words, ideas, and actions has shifted decisively. Change has ruled the intervening centuries on all continents. Any imaginative mind could continue indefinitely the roster of revolutions which have created a vast distance between the crowds Jesus addressed in Nazareth and the crowds in any contemporary city.

It is not this distance, however, which creates the hermeneutical problem; it is the corollary drawn from it. The corollary is this: Jesus' commands no longer mean the same thing, and therefore obedience to them cannot be measured by the same actions. Because of the changed situation, what appears to be obedience to a decree, like "Lay not up treasures on earth," may actually constitute disobedience. Loyalty to Jesus requires that a modern person regard his commands as no longer viable. All efforts to shape life in the twentieth century by models drawn from the first are bound not only to fail, but even to produce results opposite the intended ones. It is loyalty to truth, then, which demands that such efforts be abandoned. The changed situation has made obsolete the requirements set down by Jesus. Any reluctance to jettison those requirements is tantamount to a rebellion against the God who has placed us in cultural situations so remote from Jesus as to make obedience to his teaching virtually treasonable. When men come of age they must accept more responsibility for defining their own duty.

Such are the outlines of a standpoint which is very prevalent today. One must grant that there are impressive grounds for it, grounds all the more impressive when advanced by Christian thinkers of the highest stature. If the only alternative is the opposite extreme, an inflexible and mechanical literalism in defining the commands and an externalistic standard in measuring obedience, we would be forced to take this option. Moreover, the standpoint is stronger when one considers only the externals of the action commanded; it becomes weaker when one begins to concentrate upon the implicit context of the command, the understanding of God and man which the command embodies. Has God's character and concern for men changed so radically as to make obsolete his one-time purpose? Has the soul of man altered, or the interdependence of men in social groups been modified? Have the conditions of mental, physical, and spiritual health become so new as to render ancient wisdom archaic? The basic problem here is,

I believe, christological. Has the change in human culture been such as to undermine the authority of Jesus to disclose the truth about God's will and about man's obligations under God? Is trust no longer justified in his mission to men, including his disclosure of their duty? No one can deny the changes in the context and course of cultural life; but those changes may make more significant, rather than less, the continuities provided by the faithfulness of God to his purposes and promises vis-à-vis his creation. The process of history not only separates us from God's ancient people; it also links us to it. It is no conservative theologian, but a secular historian who writes:

> If human nature and human institutions changed completely with every decade or every generation, the study of history would be equally useless, since it would have no contact with existing realities. But our lives are based on the assumption that, while change is inevitable, it will never be complete.[6]

I have briefly analyzed the four obstacles which confront us in the course of this study. I do not wholly reject the evidence or the arguments used to sustain the four attitudes. In dealing with them, however, it is the part of wisdom to recognize two things: (1) they cannot be surmounted by argument, by logic, or by demonstration, inasmuch as they have to do with subjective evaluations of the temporal process, with group mentality, and with individual choice; (2) they are more difficult either to prove or to disprove in the large than in the small. They illustrate the penchant for dealing with gargantuan topics and for dabbling in glittering generalities. They assume that a single mind in a single process of thought can recall the records of Jesus' teaching, can appraise the changes which have transpired since his day, can avoid the obsessions and fads of our own parochial situation, and can arrive at dependable verbal solutions which do justice to all factors. But the problems of authority, compounded by the problems of translating

[6] J. R. Strayer, ed., *The Interpretation of History* (Princeton: Princeton University Press, 1943), p. 17.

ancient language into modern equivalents, do not readily yield to formulaic solutions. Less grandiose procedures may in the end be more conducive to good judgment. In the chapters which follow I have therefore turned away from inclusive generalizations and have determined to focus upon selected texts and teachings. In each case we must recall the processes of change which supervened between the origin of a command and its various literary versions, and appraise the credibility of the claim that it represents in a dependable fashion some aspect of the message of Jesus. We shall see to what extent the authority to command was yoked with the authority to disclose, i.e., the extent to which theological truth is intrinsic to the command.

Since this is not a comprehensive coverage of his message, I have not analyzed all of Jesus' commands, but have concentrated on demands which he levied upon his followers, not on the general public. I have preferred those teachings which have been neglected in recent discussion, yet which are significant pointers to the basic structure of Jesus' thought. My choice is limited to commands which, if not pristine records of Jesus' requirements, are at least authentic echoes of those requirements. The chosen teachings reveal successive stages in transmission, stages which enable us to evaluate the impact of Jesus' outlook upon successive situations and to judge the extent to which those stages pervert or destroy the earlier content. A large enough sampling permits at the end a set of generalizations which may carry weight as representative of Jesus' whole message. Rather than limiting my findings to those safe and obvious points which can be fully documented, I am willing to risk conjectural conclusions. Readers will, I hope, come to see that these conjectures have been derived from the texts themselves and not prompted by idiosyncratic desires.

Repentance and Its Corollaries

As an example of the objectives of this study and of obstacles inherent in it, let us now briefly consider the command: Repent! In all three Synoptic Gospels the preaching of Jesus begins with that demand. The act of repentance is the first step historically; it is also the first logically and psychologically. It constitutes the presupposition of the other demands, for they are addressed primarily to those who have obeyed this demand. It is in fact the implications and ramifications of repentance that the other demands spell out. This command marks the boundary between followers of Jesus and all other persons.

The preponderance of evidence makes it virtually certain that the work of John the Baptist focused upon his call to Israel to repent (Mark 1:4; Matt. 3:2; Luke 3:3). Nor should it be doubted that Jesus took over that same mission, even though the call to repent does not appear often in the Gospels. Unless the accounts of apostolic preaching are wholly misleading, this same demand was central to it (Acts 2:38; 3:19; 8:22; 17:30; 26:18-20). Mark considers the issuing of this demand as a direct and intended sequel of Jesus' commission (6:12). Thus from the earliest emergence of this prophetic movement, the call to repentance was a dominant motif. We may not doubt, therefore, that Jesus' proclamation gave prominence to this command. I know of no modern scholar who challenges its basic authenticity. Nor are there many who explicitly deny its continuing relevance.

Such a conclusion is almost worthless, however, because we have not yet considered a single tangible clue as to the precise denotation of the word in Jesus' day, nor what action might represent full obedience to it. The term remains an empty cipher until we grasp the constellation of ideas within which this idea belonged, the modes of communication by which the command was expressed, and the kinds of action which it was designed to produce. Repentance is a simple word; its meaning is anything but simple. Let us not suppose, then, that our own prior ideas of repentance are accurate enough to convey the full meaning.

Nor should we suppose that the notion and the action of repentance are found only where the word occurs. Both may be present where we might completely overlook them, were we to look only for the verbal symbol. Nevertheless, in a study such as this it is wise to consider first those texts in which the word appears. These texts are infrequent in the Synoptics; they do not form a natural sequence, nor do they betray evidence of successive stages. It is assumed in each instance that the audience knows what the word means, this vocabulary being the current coin. The command is embodied in many different forms of tradition: proverbs, paradigms, parables, historical analogies, editorial summaries. However, unlike many of the teachings of Jesus, these forms seem to have developed independently of one another, apart from the possible exception of the sermons in Acts. Our chief help in penetrating to the core of the matter will therefore be found less in tracing the history of a particular form than in reconstructing the structure of ideas within which the command belonged and on which its meaning depended.

In Mark and Matthew, repentance is a decisive, pivotal action on the part of men in response to a current and expected action on the part of God, announced by a prophet who has been sent to Israel on this very errand. This at least can be inferred from the key verses in Mark: "Jesus came into Galilee, preaching the gospel of God, and saying,

1. the time is fulfilled,
2. the kingdom of God is at hand;
3. repent,
4. believe in the gospel." *(1:14, 15.)*

In his analysis of forms, Bultmann has judged that this is a summary, phrased in Mark's own terms, of the entire message of Jesus to his compatriots.[7] It should not be taken as an accurate transcript of any specific message of Jesus. In that judgment I concur. Yet even though the verses are viewed as the literary work of an editor, they should be taken seriously as a summary of Jesus' message to Israel. They provide

[7] Rudolf Bultmann, *The History of the Synoptic Tradition,* trans. John Marsh (New York: Harper & Row, 1963), p. 341.

a clear epitome of the structure of ideas within which the idea of repentance belonged. Let us be more specific:

Lines 1-4 are obviously in Mark's thought the gist of "the gospel of God." Moreover, they represent the purpose of Jesus' coming to Galilee.

Lines 1-4 display instructive symmetry. Two assertions are followed by two commands. The assertions disclose God's action, the commands anticipate men's response. The sequence expresses an interdependence of those actions.

What can we say about the dependence of lines 3 and 4 on lines 1 and 2? Do we have a chiasmus in which line 3 depends on line 2 and line 4 on line 1? Or does 3 follow 1 and 4 follow 2; so that repentance is to be viewed as man's response to the bad news of approaching judgment (the time is fulfilled) and belief viewed as response to the good news of approaching redemption (the Kingdom is at hand)?

The relation of the two commands to the authority of the messenger is left undefined, but it seems obvious that only if Jesus' coming and his preaching are grounded in true knowledge of the time and the Kingdom do the imperatives make sense. Any action of repentance presupposes that knowledge; or we might say that it is the action of repentance that expresses and embodies that knowledge. In fact, the second command is probably prior psychologically to the first, for repentance is based on belief in the good news and in this case reflects trust in this particular prophet. Moreover, just as the action of trust produces the action of repentance, so the action of God in fulfilling the time embraces the whole sequence: the sending and coming of the herald, the delivery of his message to Galilee, the emergence of trust in him and his message, and the action of repentance. We are dealing not with a single detachable notion, but with a configuration of ideas, with interlocking girders. We may, in fact, distinguish at least eight structural ideas, locked together:

the time as being fulfilled
the approach of God's Kingdom
God's work of judgment
his offer of salvation

Jesus' warning
his promise
man's repentance
his trust.

None of these eight is self-explanatory; the sense of each is problematic. The path toward comprehension of any item runs through the comprehension of all in their mutual coherence.

Since we are at the moment concerned with the call to repentance, we may well survey other texts which expand on its meaning. One mode of expansion comes by way of an appeal to analogous moments in history. Most recent of these moments was the prophetic work of John the Baptist and the popular response. John had called men, in fleeing from the coming wrath, to make a public confession of sins and to produce appropriate deeds. So drastic was the axe's stroke, so certain the fall of every evil tree, that all normal alibis had become obsolete. Sons of Abraham had become sons of vipers, so that only a radical transformation of behavior would enable them to escape the winnowing fan (Luke 3:1-14; Matt. 3:1-10). Luke found other current examples of impending judgment in the collapse of the tower of Siloam and in the outburst of Pilate's cruelty. These examples underscored the assurance that no one was exempt from the risk of total loss, and therefore from the threat: "Unless you repent you will all likewise perish" (Luke 13:1-5). Jesus also used earlier episodes in Israel's history as analogies: the great flood, the fall of Sodom, the destruction of Egypt and Tyre, and especially the preaching of Jonah in Nineveh. Because of the greatness of Jesus' work, the unrepentance of Bethsaida was much more damning than the traditional obtuseness of Tyre and Sidon. This implied that by virtue of their public response, whole cities as cities were destroyed or vindicated on the day of judgment (Matt. 11:20-24). Jesus translated the force of this conviction into dire threats: "It shall be more tolerable on the day of judgment for the land of Sodom than for you" (Matt. 11:24). Whether an ancient episode illustrated repentance (Nineveh) or recalcitrance (Egypt), it proved useful as the basis of appeal to this "evil and adulterous generation" (Matt. 12:38-42). These illustrations reflect the conviction that sin is deeply embedded in corporate structures and that accordingly repentance is much more than occasional private remorse for trivial impieties. They also show how closely repentance is linked to acceptance of a prophet's authority (Luke 10:13-16). Response to the prophet's demand is viewed as decisive for the whole future of a community, for it would be either exalted to heaven or brought down to Hades (Matt. 11:23).

Although these analogies indicate the drastic results of the action, they tell us little concerning what precise deeds are required. For that we must look elsewhere. Do we get much help from the typical gestures which often accompanied repentance, the wearing of gunnysacks, the dusting of the face with ashes? (Matt. 11:21). Not very much. It is true that these gestures were potent symbols, which implied a rejection of normal wealth, prestige, and cultural securities, along with an acceptance of poverty, meekness, and vulnerability to ridicule. Yet they do not spell out in detail the concrete changes in social behavior which repentance required. Even so, we should not minimize the results of this survey thus far.

We have seen that repentance was a profoundly communal and eschatological decision which accompanied the movement through the doorway into a new world. By providing a prophetic revealer and leader, God has enabled men to see themselves in a new light, and to look out upon a new worldscape. In their poverty and self-humiliation, as symbolized perchance by sackcloth and ashes, they have become members of a new community. The realities of transcendent judgment and mercy have provided ample reasons for fasting and feasting. If former securities have evaporated, new reliances have emerged. Trust and fear, joy and sorrow are twin products of the message that the kingdom of God is at hand. To be sure, the validity of the message is joined to the credibility of the prophet, and the works of the prophet, which support such credibility, serve as a test of vision rather than as objective proofs. To Nineveh Jonah's word was sufficient, and to Sheba's queen, Solomon's wisdom. But to evil and adulterous progeny, even more impressive signs failed to convey conviction (Matt. 12:38-42). In short, as we glance back at the eight structural girders of the Gospel in Mark 1:15, we find all of them essential to the explication of repentance, and all of them ambiguous.

The fuzziness of meaning in all of them defeats the effort to define any one in isolation. Yet the combination of the eight in fact helps to exclude some inadequate definitions of each. What, for example, does repentance mean? Is it primarily a sense of guilt, a haunting awareness of individual inferiority and failure? No, that is inadequate to these contexts. Is it a feeling of remorse for specific misdeeds in the past? Or does it denote those deeds of penance by which a person seeks to clear the blotches from his record? Such definitions are strangely alien to the Gospel context. Is it a process of conversion from one religion to another, or from no religion to Christianity? This comes closer, but is still far off the mark. The core meaning remains basically uncertain. Perhaps that meaning cannot be conveyed by the usual dictionary definition: "Repentance is. . . ." Too many components of meaning must be considered. Some of these are theological (conceptions of God's judging and saving work), some are eschatological (conceptions of the present moment in its relation to the coming Kingdom), some are christological (views of the authority and activity of Jesus), and some are ecclesiological (the communal dimensions in the action of repentance). Each student faces this dilemma: he must reconstruct the perspective as a whole to understand the bearing of any single command, yet it is only by way of listening to specific commands that access is provided to that perspective.

It is premature now to carry further our analysis of these components, but we should not forget several implications of the passages dealing with repentance. Such passages in every case presuppose that God's action precedes man's action, and that God's action embodies an overarching concern and design for Israel. God's action is such that it discloses a chasm between his ways and man's, between his mercy and his people's hardness of heart. To him alone belong the right and the power to judge and redeem. Because sons of Abraham have forfeited their sonship through their self-deception, they must be called back to their heritage by a revealer-prophet. The Israel which repents becomes again continuous with Abraham and his legitimate heirs, along with Nineveh and the Queen of Sheba. The Israel which says No makes itself continuous with Sodom and Egypt. In other words, the action of repentance determines the existence or nonexistence of this community. By confronting a new future, with its threat and promise, men participate in God's action of creating a new world, a new age. He delivers them from the coming wrath, and opens doors to health, peace, and joy. This joy "over one sinner who repents" (Luke 15:10) is not postponed to a distant time or realm; it is realized in a realm with which the penitent community keeps very close contact. Thus the demand for repentance is creative of a new self in a new society, heavenly in origin yet earthly in manifestation. The world which men enter by this door has its own compass readings, its own latitudes and longitudes, its own modes of measuring space and time. Yet there is a terrible danger in constructing such sentences as those in this paragraph. These generalizations have too much glitter and not enough of the dull substance of ordinary human experience. The more we attempt to do justice to the initial world of thinking, the vaguer each of the ideas becomes. We may get a valid impression of the decisive significance of repentance, and yet be farther than ever from understanding what acts constitute that repentance. Vagueness at this point invites sentimental evasions of the demand, and it is this vagueness that the following chapters will seek to dissipate.

I shall select those commands which are least vague, and analyze each to see how it developed in different stages as it was applied to successive situations. Having defined specific forms of behavior, I shall try to discern the implications of that behavior for theological outlook. Will essential features of the command "Repent and believe" emerge, as we trace fruits of such faith and penitence in the life of the early churches? The thesis to be tested is: The term repentance covers all those attitudes and actions by which the community of Jesus' followers, in response to his commands, prepared itself for God's judgment and Kingdom. Its response to his authority became the incarnation of repentance and trust. Such obedience made this community the Church.

2 Let Your Yes Be Yes

The moment you falsify the scale of truth itself all your virtues are at the service of evil and are accomplices in the work of the Evil One.

D. de Rougemont,
The Devil's Share

The first saying selected for our study[1] is the demand for honest speech, a demand that is seldom questioned and as seldom examined. There is nothing vague or ambiguous about it, and yet even during the New Testament period its meaning shifted from context to context. Some of those shifts may be recovered. At first sight this command appears to have little relation to the eight girders of Mark 1:15; it therefore offers a good test of whether on closer study we may discern such connections. So now we take up the microscope.

Concerning the command not to swear at all, but always to speak the truth, he commanded as follows: "Don't swear at all, but let your yes be yes and your no, no. Anything more than this comes from the Evil One.

This saying of Jesus as reported in Justin Martyr's Apology (I, 16, 5) is the core of a teaching which appears in a more highly developed form in three New Testament passages: Matt. 5:33-37; 23:16-22; Jas. 5:12. In all but the last named passage it is attributed to Jesus. We will examine these three

[1] This essay was first presented in honor of Prof. Gerhard Delling and was published in *Novum Testamentum* 13 (1971): 1-13.

primary texts to detect various signs of development, lines of interpretation, and modes of application.

The Sermon on the Mount

At the moment we need not decide whether in this case Justin was dependent on Matthean tradition or was in touch with an independent oral source. The most recent work on this problem adopts the former option. E. P. Sanders believes that Justin used Matthew but intentionally omitted his illustrations of forbidden oaths (Matt. 5:34*b*-35) because he "was interested only in the principle."[2] I find this explanation quite unconvincing. It is as likely that these illustrations should have been added during the development of oral tradition as that they should have been intentionally deleted during one of the redactional stages. Certainly if one starts with the Justin version as the nucleus he can readily explain the other elements as accretions. It is also significant that these examples of forbidden oaths illustrate only the prohibition. They obscure and blunt the thrust of the positive command which Justin clearly understood to be central: "always to speak the truth."

Let us examine these illustrations:

> Do not swear at all,
> either by heaven, for it is the throne of God,
> or by the earth, for it is his footstool,
> or by Jerusalem, for it is the city of the great King.
> (*Matt. 5:34b, 35.*)

These three oaths reflect typical Palestinian Jewish practice. The banning of these three appears to spring from a prudential motive: because of the divine power to enforce penalties, such oaths are too dangerous to be used. In swearing by the earth, the oath-taker might be attempting to evade divine sanctions, but such evasion was actually impossible.

[2] E. P. Sanders, *The Tendencies of the Synoptic Tradition* (New York: Cambridge University Press, 1969), pp. 57, 67.

A still different rationale appears in the fourth example of oaths which should be avoided.

> Do not swear by your head,
> for you cannot make one hair white or black.
> (*Matt. 5:36.*)

It is the futility of swearing which becomes the point here. To swear by one's own head carries no force, inasmuch as a person has no power to change one hair from black to white. One may also discern an implicit warning to the creditor that he should not trust another's oath. Both notions are alien to the thought of vs. 37, although one can understand how, once the saying of 34*a,* 37 was current in oral tradition, it would attract examples of oaths like these, some representing danger to the debtor (34*b,* 35), some to the creditor (36). One may conclude that these additions (34*b*-36) were probably made before the teaching was drawn to this Matthean context, for there were subsequent changes which are more probably Matthean.

The context in Matthew makes intelligible the addition of 5:33. There is nothing in the saying itself to suggest a necessary reference to the Leviticus law. Why should the command for transparently honest speech be contrasted with the law against perjury? It was presumably the combination of six antitheses in Matthew which dictated not only the introductory formula but also the citation of a specific law (Lev. 19:12) to serve as a foil against which Jesus' command could be set. But the contrast between the command "to perform to the Lord what you have sworn" and the command to avoid oaths altogether is awkward and imperfect. Three of Matthew's antitheses repudiate or abrogate an earlier law (5:31-32, 38-39, 43-44). Not so the saying on oaths. Like the commands on murder and adultery (5:21-22, 27-28), this command affirms the earlier law and then goes on to assert a more rigorous standard. It may well be that these three—the prohibition of anger, lust, and deceit—formed a pre-Matthean trilogy which the evangelist arbitrarily combined at a later date with the three other antitheses—on divorce, nonresistance, love of enemy.

In summary, I believe that the Matthean version preserves the traces of four major stages in the history of this saying.

Nucleus —5:34*a*, 37—an oral tradition, highly memorable and widely current.

Stage 1 —the addition of 34*b*, 35, three examples of oaths to illustrate the negative half of the command. These examples were included from a very early date, perhaps during the oral stage.

Stage 2 —the addition of 36, a fourth example, with a different reason for not swearing.

Stage 3 —the addition of 33 and simultaneously the fusion with the prohibition of anger and lust into a trilogy, perhaps illustrating 5:20 and possibly linked to 6:2-6, 16-18 (cf. below, pp. 47 ff.). If one posits the existence of M, a pre-Matthean written source of material peculiar to Matt., this trilogy probably belonged to it.

Stage 4 —the addition of the other three antitheses into a series of six illustrations of 5:17, to serve as a far-reaching definition of the ethic of the church as opposed to the ethic of the synagogue. This was probably a major step in the composition of the Sermon and of the entire Gospel.

Obviously each of these stages affects the motivation and application of the nuclear command. The later stages alter the motivation so that it comes to be centered upon the contrast between the new and the old commands, i.e., between church and synagogue. The earlier changes suggest that the primary objective was an attack upon swearing. The negative "swear not at all" becomes the operative element in the nucleus. But when we ask of the tripartite nucleus whether the accent originally fell on the ban against oaths or on the radical honesty of all utterance, preference should clearly be given to the latter alternative. Oaths are mentioned merely because their use implies that the speaker's word is not as good as his deed, that others need some protection against his tendency to lie, and that he would be forced by an oath to fulfill pledges when without it he might default. Obedience to the positive command would render obsolete any reliance on oaths, along with many other forms of assuring the validity of promises. The nucleus by itself, prior to the accretions, focuses attention on the source, the heart, and on that complex of desires which impels a person to speak.

> What Jesus envisages here is a state of affairs in which oaths, cross-examinations, and punishments for perjury are alike unnecessary, because a man's word is enough: because, in other words, he can be trusted to tell the truth. . . . Truthfulness has become in his sight more precious than any seeming advantage that might be gained by falsehood.[3]

The Attack on Hypocrisy in Matthew 23

Another version of the teaching appears in Matt. 23:16-22, although with none of the three constituents apparent. Here there is no total ban on oaths, no positive command for honesty, and no reference to swearing as a product of the desire to deceive. Yet there are links between the two passages which may be found in the secondary elements. Both passages are part of a far-reaching hostility between the church and the synagogue, or, more precisely, between the disciples and the Pharisees. In both passages we find the oath by heaven as the throne of God, while the oath by the temple in 23:16 is comparable to that by the holy city in 5:35. The rationale of the verses is clarified when we set them in couplet form and rearrange them slightly.

> 1*a* Whoever swears by the temple is not bound,
> 1*b* but whoever swears by the temple gold is bound.
>
> 2*a* Whoever swears by the altar is not bound,
> 2*b* but whoever swears by the gift on it is bound.

We are obviously dealing with highly developed casuistry in oath-making. Where verbal oaths provide the chief bond of security, the precise location and accessibility of the surety become important. The scribal interpreters of the Torah are

[3] T. W. Manson, *The Teaching of Jesus* (New York: Cambridge University Press, 1963), p. 298.

accused of teaching that one set of oaths, e.g., the temple, the altar, is not binding, presumably because, if a debtor defaults, his creditor cannot place a lien on the surety. The other set of oaths is binding because the gold or the gift on the altar can be seized in compensation for broken pledges. The assumption on which this scribal casuistry is based is shown to be faulty, first by two rhetorical questions (1*cd*, 2*cd*) and then by a positive declaration (2*ef*, 1*ef*).

1*c* Which is more sacred:
1*d* the gold or the temple which sanctifies it?

2*c* Which is more sacred:
2*d* the gift or the altar which sanctifies it?

2*e* Whoever swears by the altar
2*f* swears by it and by everything on it.

1*e* Whoever swears by the temple
1*f* swears by it and (everything in it).

The two questions are framed to match each other (synonymous parallelism) and to contradict the assumptions on which the scribes declared some oaths to be binding and others not to be. The last four couplets are arranged in a chiastic sequence: temple—altar—altar—temple. The last two constitute the declaration which is set against the scribal principle;

2*ef* are antithetically parallel to 2*ab*
1*ef* are set over against 1*ab*.

The intent appears to be to exclude distinctions among oaths by reference to the object (e.g., the altar, the gift) in order to make it more difficult to swear with impunity and to increase the dangers and penalties of perjury. Undoubtedly this modification moves in the direction of excluding all such casuistry, but it falls far short of the rigor of Matt. 5:34*a*, 37.

In the last two couplets another principle is introduced:

(1*e*) 3*a* Whoever swears by the temple
(1*f*) 3*b* swears by it and by him who dwells there.

4*a* Whoever swears by heaven
4*b* swears by God's throne and by him who sits there.

It is interesting to see how the couplet *3ab* was formed in such a way as to bridge the gap between two separate teachings. *3a* is shaped to match *2e* to complete the example of 1*abcd*. It would make that foregoing structure perfectly symmetrical if *3b* had read, as we have edited it in 1*f*, " (the temple) and everything in it." But *3ab* also is parallel to *4ab*. It is this symmetry which requires the phrase "by him who dwells there." These last two couplets add a new motif, a motif which was prominent at one stage in the history of 5:33-37. All oaths directly or indirectly appeal to God; all are therefore binding, since they call on him to guarantee their fulfillment. The breaking of any oath, however minimal the stakes, therefore invites a maximum penalty. No protection should be sought by verbal deftness in choosing specific stakes. Those who rely upon such deftness, following the guidance of the blind scribes, deceive only themselves and will ultimately be caught in their own trap.

This is a fascinating unit of catechetical material. It almost certainly antedates the destruction of the temple, because after that even such oaths became useless. It belongs within a Palestinian Jewish environment in which scribal teachings still carried presumptive authority. It was shaped and used at a time when competition was still acute between the scribal leaders of the church and those of the synagogue. The argument is typical of rabbinic styles of thought and expression. It could conceivably refer back to debates between Jesus and the scribes. Attribution to Jesus becomes difficult, however, when we notice that the outlook in this pericope in Matt. 23:16-22 actually enforces the principle enunciated in Matt. 5:33, which was there explicitly set aside by Jesus: "You shall not swear falsely, but shall perform to the Lord what you have sworn."

The Version in James

Still another primary version of the teaching appears in the Epistle of James 5:12:

Above all, my brethren, do not swear, either by heaven or by earth or with any other oath, but let your yes be yes and your no be no, that you may not fall under condemnation.

This is undoubtedly the same teaching, even though it is not attributed to Jesus in this epistle. Present is the tripartite form which we noticed in Justin and identified as the nucleus. The negative ban which Justin expressed by the adverb *holos* is illustrated by three examples (as in Matt. 5:34*b,* 35) of which two (heaven or earth) are specific, while the third (any other oath) seems to cover all conceivable examples. This latter may also be the intent of Matt. 5:36, since swearing by one's own hair is the most trivial oath conceivable. The positive injunction coincides almost exactly with the wording as found in Justin. Although the reason given for the command (condemnation) differs from that in Justin (the Evil One), it is not alien, for it was axiomatic that every human thought or action which the devil fathered would be condemned by God in the final judgment. James provides a third witness to the fact that the command for absolute honesty in speech, with the corresponding rejection of oaths, had become recognized in the New Testament church as the norm of behavior. The James version also indicates that a high respect was accorded to this norm ("above all, my brethren," 5:12). Whether any inferences may be safely drawn from the Jamesian context is problematical. The teaching may have been attracted to this point by the similarities to 5:9 and to the danger of condemnation (cf. ἵνα μὴ κριθῆτε with ἵνα μὴ ὑπὸ κρίσιν). Transparent honesty may have seemed especially difficult and urgent as an expression of patience in the midst of persecution and suffering (5:6, 10, 13). Such contextual links are very problematic, however. It is more likely that we are dealing with an unorganized jumble of oral traditions which the editor felt no pressure to reorder into a smoother literary sequence. What is important is the internal integrity of the teaching itself, its self-sufficient completeness, its unambiguous prohibition and command, its undiminished rigor, its unquestioned affinity both to the outlook of Jesus and to the standards accepted under very difficult circumstances by the church during its first decades.

It is not my purpose to determine whether there were literary connections between the texts in Justin, Matt. 5, and James. Significantly, the basic nucleus appears, with minor modifications, in all three. There is no sure evidence that Justin and James were dependent on Matt. 5:33-37. If they were, they omitted the later and nonessential elements of that tradition, including the idea that the occasion for the teaching was Jesus' debate with the scribes rather than his concern for the integrity of his followers. More likely, each of the three writers was incorporating catechetical materials which were still circulating orally in their various communities. Of the stages in the development of Matt. 5:33-37 as outlined above, Justin's version is nearest the nucleus and James is nearest Stage 1. Not only are Justin and James free of polemics, but they find no use for the antitheses of Matt. 23, or for calculating exactly the binding force of various oaths and the corresponding dangers of perjury. Neither appears acquainted with the order of teachings in Matt. 5 or 23. Both preserve the dominant emphasis on the positive command, i.e., the condemnation applies not so much to the use of oaths as to a person's desire to deceive. In terms of primitiveness, I believe that James and Justin have preserved an earlier form of the command than Matthew has. This form is oriented directly toward the eschatological judgment. Any deviation from truthfulness in speech, any desire to use speech to deceive another person, is fathered by the devil and/or places the speaker under God's final judgment. The converse is also true. Each victory over the devil by way of mastering deceit demonstrates the ingressive power of God's Kingdom.

Some Cognate Teachings

But let us return to our major concern. I maintain that the nuclear teaching is in full accord with standards adopted by the early church. That accord may be adequately documented by the following assortment of six passages.

1.

1 You brood of vipers! How can you speak good when you are evil?
2 For out of the abundance of the heart the mouth speaks.

3 The good man out of his good treasure brings forth good,
4 The evil man out of his evil treasure brings forth evil.

5 On the day of judgment men will render account for every careless word they utter.
6 For by your words you will be justified,
7 And by your words you will be condemned.

(*Matt. 12:34-37.*)

Because of the absence of any reference to swearing, we seldom associate this passage with the others we have examined. Yet we should remember that the nuclear version was tripartite. Here, in fact, two of those parts appear in developed form: speech is a test of inner integrity, and every instance of deceitful speech receives condemnation. An absolute mutuality between the heart and the mouth is affirmed in the first four lines. Matthew has again placed these lines in the context of Jesus' battle with the scribes (cf. 5:20; 23:16). Apart from line 1, however, they might have been addressed to his disciples. Intrinsically, the saying applies to all forms of speech and not simply to scribal slanders against Jesus. The "careless word" of 12:36 performs the same function as the "hairs" of Matt. 5:36 and the "any other oath" of Jas. 5:12; by using the trivial instance, the casual, useless word, the principle is made all the more absolute. Even though Matthew applies this argument to enemies of the church, it would carry little weight with Christians unless they had already accepted it as applying to themselves. This inference is amply supported by another Matthean logion:

2.

What comes out of the mouth proceeds from the heart, and this defiles a man.
For out of the heart come evil thoughts, murder, adultery, fornication, theft, false witness, slander.
These are what defile a man.

(*Matt. 15:18-20a.*)

This teaching argues for a similar unity between mouth and heart, a similar concern for tracing each sin to its origin. It is true that not all the sins mentioned emerge from the mouth, but three do: evil disputings, false testimonies, and blasphemings. These are not alien to the sins of duplicity and dishonest speech banned by our nuclear saying. The context in Matt. 15 applies the requirement of integrity to the controversy over defilement. Apart from that context, however, there would be a much more inclusive reference for the logion, and we may well assume that in oral tradition the more inclusive reference would have been preserved.

3. If we focus attention on the third element in our original saying—"Anything more than this comes from the Evil One" —we find many texts which strike a similar accent. This clause says something about the origin of the desire to deceive; it also says something about the devil. The activity of the devil is to be located most surely at the source of the stream of deceit, the heart (Matt. 13:19). The devil is the father of lies. He who does evil proves by that deed that he is born of the Evil One (I John 3:12). When Ananias lied to the apostles, Peter said, "Why has Satan filled your heart to lie to the Holy Spirit?" (Acts 5:3.) In other writings it is said that the world constitutes that realm which has been deceived by him (Rev. 12:9). That world is not separable from the heart.

4. The paraenetic sections of Ephesians are representative of the standards of speech which were accepted widely in the early church. Here it is axiomatic that birth into the new humanity required the cessation of lying and the adoption of truthful speaking (Eph. 4:25). To return to deceitful and angry speech would be "to give opportunity to the devil" (4:27). The type of speech a person uses discloses what is in fact his relationship to the old and the new creation, to the Holy Spirit (4:30), and to the wrath of God (5:6).

5. These new standards concerning honest speech were seen to be especially incumbent on teachers and apostles. James 3 is an impressive collection of aphorisms concerning the dangers confronting the tongue of the teacher. Especially vulnerable is the teacher to the duplicity of allowing the same mouth to voice blessing and cursing. Such a practice provokes a question which is entirely akin to that of Matt. 5:37—"Does a spring pour forth from the same opening fresh water and brackish?" (Jas. 3:11.) In several of his letters Paul insists that truthful speech is a necessary tool of the apostle (II Cor. 6:7), and he is greatly incensed by any attack upon his own integrity (I Thess. 2:1-6).

6. In connection with his defense against the charges of compromises and equivocation ("ready to say yes and no at once"), Paul turned the debate into a christological confession:

> For the Son of God, Jesus Christ . . . was not Yes and No; but in him it is always Yes. For all the promises of God find their Yes in him. That is why we utter the Amen through him, to the glory of God. *(II Cor. 1:19, 20.)*

In this remarkable confession there converge several of the ultimate presuppositions of the command issued by Jesus to his followers: "Let your yes be yes and your no, no." God is the source and guardian of perfect trustworthiness and integrity. His promises are absolutely sure. The Christian has found this truth fully vindicated in Christ. In him there is no mixing of truth with falsehood. Through him the Christian voices his own Amen. Faith, therefore, should eliminate any tendency to use evasive and deceptive speech. To waver, to vacillate, to hide one's real intentions is to say yes and no at once; that kind of equivocation is the mark of living according to the flesh (κατὰ σάρκα, II Cor. 1:17). Paul is fully aware that God is the witness of whatever he says (1:23), an indication that he feared God's judgment only (cf. Jas. 5:12, "lest you fall under condemnation").

These six passages provide ample documentation for concluding that every element in our nuclear saying was indigenous to the outlook of the early church as a whole. The ruthless rigor of that saying is preserved in many different literary traditions with a minimum of accommodation to less rigid standards of honesty. There is also evidence that this command was never considered to be of casual or secondary concern. It could not have been deleted from the catechesis without damaging the whole ethos of the new humanity. Moreover, it would be wrong to limit its sphere to moral theology, for it was directly related to basic kerygmatic and dogmatic concerns, such as the following:

The conception of God as the source, judge, and vindicator of truthful speech;

the conception of Satan as a power who opposes God by encouraging men to shape their speech by self-serving rather than God-serving desires;

the conception of Christ as the measure and vindicator of God's sincerity and power;

the conception of the Spirit as active in the community and in its members, and as being "grieved" whenever a believer made the slightest effort to deceive;

the conception of the self, in which destiny is determined by the heart and by what emerges from it;

an evaluation of words not by their effect on society but by their origin in the heart, by whether their paternity is God or the devil;

an eschatology in which final judgment serves to disclose the primordial state of the heart from which all words and deeds have come;

an ethic which understands the demands of God as directly embedded in a man's heart and as tested by every word which that man speaks to his neighbor.

Thus far the scope of our study has been limited to early Christian literature. If we were to broaden this scope we could multiply relevant evidence. We must be content here with noting a number of similar teachings by the Jewish rabbis. That the use of "Yes" and "No" to indicate integrity of character was not unusual is shown by this saying of Rabbi Huna: "The Yes of the righteous is Yes, and their No is No." [4] Another rabbinic aphorism reminds us of two of the three elements in Jas. 5:12:

He who punished the generations of the Flood and the Tower of Babel will also punish him who does not keep his word. Let your Yes and No both be righteous. Do not speak with your mouth what you do not mean in your heart.[5]

One might say that the conscience of every loyal Jew was characterized by his awareness that God discerns and punishes every intention to deceive; he "shall judge the secret things and none shall be able to utter a lying word before him" (I Enoch 49:4). Speech to one's brother thus becomes a way of disclosing one's relation to God:

He who deceives or lies to man is as if he deceives or lies to God.[6]

Many Jewish rabbis were far from superficial in their analysis of the implications of falsehood. To bear false witness is tantamount, they said, to the declaration that God did not create the world.[7] A whole theology, cosmology, and anthropology are reflected by such an aphorism. Any dishonest word, even when supported by an oath, discloses an atheistic view of the self and the world. This is even clearer in the statement, " 'Thou shalt not bear false witness' corresponds to 'let us make man in our own image.' " [8]

Consideration of such examples of Jewish teaching should make us suspicious of the polemic which induced the addition of Matt. 5:33 to the earlier tradition of Jesus' command. On the other hand, these examples do not diminish the force of

[4] Ruth R. VII, 6, as given in Montefiore and Loewe, *A Rabbinic Anthology*, #1087.

[5] Baba Mezia IV, 2:49*a*, as cited in Montefiore and Loewe in *ibid.*, #1088.

[6] Sifre Numbers, Naso Par. 2, f.2*a*, as in Montefiore and Loewe in *ibid.*, #1078.

[7] Jerusalem Talmud, Berakoth I.8, f.3*c*, line 24.

[8] Pesikta Rabbati 108*a*, *b*, as in Montefiore and Loewe, *A Rabbinic Anthology*, #1092.

that nuclear command. They may, in fact, reinforce its strategic significance. Innovation is not essential to truth. It is quite possible to find in the time of Jesus the prohibition of swearing by the Essenes for much the same reason as that given by Jas. 5:12:

> Swearing is avoided by them and they esteem it worse than perjury, for they say that he who cannot be believed without (swearing by) God is already condemned. (Josephus, *War, II, 8:6.*)

Implications

An understanding of the strategic importance of the demand for honesty in the ancient world is enhanced by the investigations of Walter J. Ong, S.J., into the characteristics of an oral-aural culture as contrasted with a chirographic-typographic culture.[9] In that culture where the spoken word is the primary means of communication, power may be traced to its source in the voice. The voice, in turn, is the chief tangible key to the intangible reality of both speaker and auditor. Speech is an event, a happening in time which bridges the distance between two hidden selves, destroying the isolation of both participants. To hear another's voice locates the hearer in the midst of the happening, "in the middle of actuality and simultaneity" (p. 128). Not only does each self express itself in words, but also the interpersonal dimensions of reality come into play in the conversation. And those dimensions are hospitable to the widest conceivable range of symbolic meanings. The simplest words, like yes and no, can attract the widest penumbra of connotations. Spoken words become the essential means by which a person enters into the life-consciousness of others, and this very entrance enables him to enter into his own life (p. 15), so that in his use of words a man expresses his sense of presence to himself, to other men, to God. All this can be illustrated negatively by the crippling spiritual effects of deafness.

[9] Cf. Walter J. Ong, S.J., *The Presence of the Word* (New Haven: Yale University Press, 1967); see also his essay in *American Anthropologist* 71 (1969): 639-40.

Thus in a culture which depends on oral speech, the intrusion of the intent to deceive pollutes reality at its very source and invokes ultimate penalties on the speakers. Moreover, in such a culture a community becomes especially dependent upon the rugged integrity of its teachers. The emergence of a community in which both teachers and members accept and obey the demands of absolute trustworthiness in speech could rightly be construed as marking an eschatological transformation of the world. It is as a sign of such a transformation that we should view the early Christian emphasis on the command of Jesus: "Let your yes be yes."

Such considerations as these may throw light upon the current hermeneutical emphasis on the creative (and destructive) power of language.

> A word is dead
> When it is said,
> Some say.
>
> I say it just
> Begins to live
> That day.[10]

That is surely true of the early Christian notion of God's word. God speaks, and it is done. Jesus speaks, and demons of deceit tremble. When the call is heard, a man's yes may represent the creative work of God, mediated by a prophet who announces the fullness of time and demands repentance and trust.

So we discover several features of this teaching which are germane to the objectives of this book. First, we notice how specific this command is, how inescapably definite and immediate in its application to every person at every moment. By becoming most particular and personal, the command becomes most universal in its relevance. In dealing simultaneously with the simplest human word and with the unseen Arbiter of truth, the command introduces its hearers into a realm that is relatively immune to temporal changes in man's

[10] Emily Dickinson.

condition, in his language and forms of thought. Second, it is clear that the demand places each listener within the field of battle between God and Satan; it does this in such a way as to draw each successive situation into that same field. It is the intensity of this battle which creates moral pressure, and not the temporal distance from the *eschaton.* Third, the substance of this demand functions as a valuable aid in defining the repentance of Mark 1:15. The command identifies subservience to Satan and citizenship in his kingdom with lack of integrity in speech; it makes clear that the recovery of integrity marks a turning away from that kingdom as a result of the intrusion of Jesus' authority. "Believe in the gospel" (Mark 1:15) thus receives conceptual definition in the command and actual definition in a man's obedience to it. Finally, this teaching alerts us to the significance of what happens in the silence of man's heart, where desires emerge before they are embodied in words. It is this inner dimension which is so frequently lacking in expositions of Jesus' message, a dimension we will explore further in the following chapter.

3 Keep It Secret

Padlock your tongue, or it will lock you up.

Proverb, British Guiana

	A	B	C
1.	When you give alms	When you pray	When you fast
2.	don't be like the hypocrites	don't be like the hypocrites	don't be like the hypocrites
3.	for they sound trumpets[1] before them in the synagogues and in the streets	for they love to stand and pray in the synagogues and street corners	for they disfigure their[1] faces and look dismal
4.	that they may be praised by men	that they may be seen by men	that they may be seen by men
5.	truly I say to you	truly I say to you	truly I say to you
6.	they have their reward	they have their reward	they have their reward
7.	But when you give alms	But when you pray	But when you fast
8.	don't let your left hand know what your right is doing	go into your room and shut the door	anoint your head and wash your face
9.	so that your alms may be in secret	so that your praying[1] may be in secret	so that your fasting[1] may be in secret

[1] I have modified the text in these lines to accentuate the parallel constructions, but this has not changed the basic thought.

10. and your Father who sees in secret	10. and your Father who sees in secret	10. and your Father who sees in secret
11. will reward you	11. will reward you	11. will reward you

(*Matt. 6:2-6, 16-18.*)

We now take up the most complex poetic construction in the Sermon on the Mount and the longest, apart from the collection of six antitheses in Matt. 5:21-48. Compared with those earlier paragraphs, this structure is far more symmetrical, and the parallelisms are far more deftly articulated. Here the student finds three almost perfect examples of synonymous parallelism, each of which takes the form of a perfectly arranged antithetical parallelism.[2] This teaching in triplicate is an excellent instance of the operation of the rule of three in the shaping of oral tradition, three examples being considered sufficient to justify an unlimited extension of the basic principle to other situations. The triptych also illustrates the dexterous creation of hyperbole, along with the vivid use of both auditory (the trumpets) and visual (the doleful face) images. The very perfection of symmetry aids the student both in discerning accretions and in penetrating to the original intention in spite of accretions which obscure it. Unlike the teaching on honesty, this material appears only in the Matthean Gospel, and we are therefore forced to guess at its shape in the pre-Matthean stages. Nonetheless, the form and substance of the teaching is such as to give a measure of plausibility to these conjectures.

The three stanzas deal directly with three forms of piety which had become traditional in the Jewish milieu.[3] The

[2] There is striking unanimity among scholars in recognizing this basic structure. Cf. J. Dupont, *Les Béatitudes* (Bruges: Abbaye de Saint-André, 1958), p. 161; A. George, "La justice à faire dans le secret," *Biblica* 40 (1959): 590-98; J. O'Hara, "Christian Fasting," *Scripture* 19 (1967): 3-18.

[3] Cf. D. Daube, *The New Testament and Rabbinic Judaism* (London: University of London Press, 1956), pp. 63-64; J. O'Hara, "Christian Fasting," pp. 3 ff.; A. George, "La justice . . . ," pp. 590 ff.; M. Black, *Aramaic Approach to the Gospels and Acts* (New York: Oxford University Press, 2nd ed., 1954), pp. 133-34.

actions described were presumed to be typical of the "synagogues and the street-corners" in Israel. The teaching would have been quite ineffective had these three virtues not been status symbols which, because of public reverence, had become legitimate goals of ambitious leaders. The majority was habitually inclined to praise men who were most generous in philanthropy and most devout in prayer and fasting, and such praise was sought by the leaders as verification of their godliness. The very strength of these status symbols is reflected in the caricatures, for the charge of hypocrisy would lose its cogency apart from the realities of public veneration. It is hard for modern readers to comprehend how offensive this attack originally was, for these three types of practice have largely lost their prestige value.

This erosion of the conditions which prompted this teaching has encouraged its neglect by modern scholars. I am aware of only one essay in recent exegetical discussion (the article by A. George noted above) which has taken appropriate notice of its strategic importance for theology. Such neglect of a clear command of Jesus, triply accentuated and illustrated, can be defended only with difficulty. If the command did in fact come from Jesus, it should be viewed as a significant index of his position as a whole, for, as we shall see, the triptych carried many profound implications which reach far beyond these three forms of piety. Even if the command originated in the catechetical work of the pre-Matthean church, it retains high value as an index of the early Christian ethos, or, to use more recent jargon, style of life. However, before exploring the historical and theological ramifications, we must look more closely at the formal construction of the triple command, for it is this formal structure which must serve as a major stimulus and control of exegetical reactions. In the parallel arrangement I have arbitrarily altered the text for the purpose of stressing the skeletal structure. This chart is not the hypothetical original version, but only an abstract construction to aid in the analysis of forms. It will serve its purpose if it helps in attaining several objectives: the first, to bring to the surface five elements of symmetry, then to provide some controls for the basic interpretation of the teaching. Thereafter we can examine those elements in the Matthean edition which obscure the symmetry, and explore the origin of these elements. Finally, we will venture to appraise the significance for theology of the nuclear tryptych.

The Symmetrical Features

1. Perhaps the first thing to note is the fact that lines 1 are precisely parallel to one another and also to lines 7, except for variation in the connective particles (δὲ, καὶ, οὖν) and for the different kinds of piety. To begin six successive sentences with such similar sounds facilitates memorization and suggests an original unity of intention. There is, to be sure, a minor variation in the type of Greek clause used in lines 7, but the variation is readily explained by syntactical demands which do not alter the meaning.

2. Even more noteworthy is the complete identity in Greek of lines 5 and 6. This identity extends throughout the whole textual tradition. The recurrence of this accent establishes the unity of the triptych and also suggests some significant connections with 5:21-48, where a similar saying is used six times.[4]

3. It is impossible to overlook the congruence of lines 10 and 11 in each stanza. C 10 does, to be sure, exhibit some variation in the Greek, depending on which Mss. an editor follows, but this variation does not noticeably change the meaning. These lines are, in turn, the precise opposites of lines 5 and 6. These contrasts serve to accentuate the choice between a reward from men and a reward from the Father.

4. This option is shown to be the direct consequence of another option: the desire "to be seen and praised by men" versus the desire for the action to be in secret. Again there are verbal variations, but the impressive thing is the basic similarity of lines 9 and their equally basic opposition to lines 4. These lines represent the decisive issue, since the alternatives in lines 6 and 11 are the direct consequence of these motive-actions in lines 4 and 9.

[4] Cf. E. Klostermann, "Zum Verständnis von Matthäus 6:2," *Zeitschrift für die neutestamentliche Wissenschaft* 47 (1956) : 280.

5. There is, finally, an important similarity in lines 2 in the prohibition of hypocrisy. The similarity disappears in lines 3, but it becomes all the more prominent in lines 4. Hypocrisy is here defined as any intentional action which simultaneously seeks God's approval and man's praise. The teaching underscores not only the hypocrisy of such action, but its futility as well. Desires for human and divine praise are declared to be mutually exclusive.

Finally we notice that none of the lines in the three stanzas is expendable, although certain words may be superfluous and in a single case (vs. 17) a whole clause may be. The symmetries are bound together into a tightly knit unity which tends to resist change, whether in oral or in written transmission.

Guidelines for Interpretation

The teaching provides clear clues to the stance of both teacher and audience. A single teacher is envisaged, one who speaks with authority and knowledge. Lines 5, 6, 10, 11 take for granted that he has access to knowledge about how human and divine rewards are conferred. If men have secrets, he knows them; if God has secrets, he knows them also. He can even announce as certain the action of "your Father." The sententious character of lines 5 bespeaks an emphasis strong enough to counter any opposite assumption concerning rewards from men. It is taken for granted that the authority of this speaker rightly extends over such central religious duties as the three named, and by implication over other duties as well. Located in the Sermon on the Mount, the triptych is of course attributed to Jesus. But when one considers the status and function implicitly accorded to the speaker, it becomes virtually impossible to imagine that the early Christian church would attribute it to any other author. A. George is therefore fully justified in associating this triple command with Matt. 11:27-28 as one mode by which the Son actually disclosed his knowledge of the Father.[5]

[5] A. George, "La justice . . . ," p. 598.

Equally important inferences may be definitely drawn regarding the audience. It is assumed that this audience recognizes the right of its teacher to set the norms for their behavior. It is also assumed that they have accepted an obligation to act as loyal sons of the Father and that these filial-paternal bonds are of the most intimate and secret kind. The shift from the plurals in lines 5 to the singulars in lines 7 signifies the existence of a community in which the norms for individual behavior are established and recognized. By their nature, secret actions are highly individualized; yet this teacher is addressing a group of individuals who are bound together by their loyalty to him and by their sonship to the same father. The teaching as a whole is addressed to the whole people, yet each command can be obeyed only by each individual.[6] Hypocrites could be dealt with in the plural (lines 2); similar plurals in B 1 and C 1 may thus have been encouraged. But groups as groups cannot illustrate the secret piety of lines 7 and 8. The secrecies of sonship require the singularities of selfhood.

With a slighter degree of plausibility we may draw a further inference concerning the plural *you* of lines 5. This audience addressed by Jesus may represent the smaller band of disciples in their special role as pacesetters in piety, as the scribes and catechists of the Christian community. Matthew's Gospel, following the practice of Mark, normally distinguished the twelve disciples (mathetai) from the larger crowds (ochloi) of followers, a distinction roughly parallel to the contrast between the leaders (scribes, prophets, and wise men, 23:24) in the Matthean church and the more numerous laymen.[7] The disciples were visualized by Matthew as teachers-elect, doing their interne training under Jesus' tutelage; parallel to them were the Pharisaic leaders of the synagogues who had defaulted on their assigned duties. These interne-teachers were being indoctrinated into a higher standard of

[6] T. W. Manson, *The Teaching of Jesus,* pp. 165-66; A. George, "La justice . . . ," p. 594.

[7] Cf. my essay "Audience Criticism and Markan Ecclesiology," in B. Reicke and H. Baltensweiler, eds., *Neues Testament und Geschichte* (Tübingen and Zürich: Theologischer Verlag, 1972), pp. 79-89.

righteousness (5:19, 20) for the sake of all the sons of their Father. This hypothesis gives greater specificity to the plural *you* in lines 5, in harmony with the clues in 5:1. Even so, we need not rely on it to give full resonance to these commands by which Jesus communicated to his followers this *sine qua non* of sonship to their Father.

What inference may be drawn from the harsh reference to the hypocrites in the negative half of each stanza? The strength of these prohibitions would be proportionate to the audience desire to dissociate itself from this particular group of hypocrites. The identity of the group is entirely clear: they are models of piety in the synagogue who have succeeded in winning the veneration of the wider public. They and their admirers assume that this veneration and God's praise are entirely complementary. However, it must be noted that the command is directed neither toward the Pharisees nor toward their followers, but rather toward competing leaders and their followers. Only in these terms would the negative commands elicit a strong impulse toward obedience. Without much doubt the triptych was shaped originally in a polemical situation, where the teaching was reinforced by existing hostility toward a group of "hypocrites" whose authority over communal behavior has been repudiated.[8]

This polemical feature, however, can easily be misconstrued. The teaching is not in itself a weapon to be used in warfare against the Pharisees, who, incidentally, are not mentioned. The whole accent falls rather on the positive behavior of Jesus' own followers. The triptych was shaped to secure pedagogical rather than polemic results. The supreme danger and the alternative opportunity are those which confront Christ's disciples. The central thrust is directed toward producing a piety which is wholly secret. To seek superiority over the Pharisees would be as dubious a contradiction of lines 7-11 as to seek public recognition for one's goodness. The command aims at behavior that would make quite unthinkable the comparative judgments on which hypocrisy thrives and without which it dies. Individuals cannot obey this triple de-

[8] Cf. O'Hara, "Christian Fasting," pp. 3-4.

mand and continue either to seek or to claim superiority over their religious adversaries. The fact that they continue that practice is evidence only of the continued relevance of the appeal, "Don't continue to be like the hypocrites."

The exegete may also easily misconstrue the polemic as a weapon in the struggle between religious institutions. He may infer that Jesus here repudiated the Jewish practices and forms in favor of alternative Christian forms (cf. Didache XI). But the three stanzas in themselves, excluding of course vss. 7-15, do not support this. In fact, they assume that hypocrites cannot be distinguished from non-hypocrites merely by reference to varying forms or practices. They nowhere require the existence of separate Christian forms or practices. Moreover, they neither support the iconoclastic repudiation of these pious practices nor insist on their observance by all disciples. The only presupposition in this regard is conveyed by the conditional clause, "When you give alms. . . ." The character of obedience is such that it cannot be detected or measured either by opposition to all public praying, charity, and fasting, or by the cultivation of these. Rather, by repudiating all group estimates of holiness, this triad is equally destructive of both reactionary and revolutionary programs. Or to put the same truth conversely, it is impossible for any religious community or institution to grant to any individual the slightest degree of immunity from this prohibition of hypocrisy or from this command to secrecy. The reason for this is made perfectly clear by the structure itself in the decisive importance which it gives to lines 4 and 9:

> that they may be seen by men . . . ,
> that your praying may be in secret . . . .

The inescapable issue for every person with respect to his own situation, whatever that may be in terms of formal religious affiliation, is the choice between these two desires, followed by their embodiment in appropriate action. The chief control, then, which the structure exerts on exegesis is this: exegesis, if it is to fit this text, must focus upon the manifest intent of the teaching to incite this desire and this action on the part of this audience.

Developments in the Tradition

The structural integrity of this triple teaching forces the reader to respect its penetrating radicalism. In a sense no further exegesis is needed, since the primary truth is stated so simply and so clearly. Interpretation may only obscure the threat and the thrust. That is in fact what has happened with the successive accretions. We should now deal with some of these, and first of all with several variants in the text which can be assigned rather confidently to post-Matthean dates.

The meaning is altered substantially by a variant that comes at the end of lines 11: "your Father who sees in secret will reward you *openly*." A large number of early Mss. give this reading, although most modern translations rightly reject it. One reason for rejection is that it mistakes the logic which is built into the three stanzas. When this adverb "openly" is added, the major antithesis is located in the contrast between the hiddenness of the action in lines 10 and the publicity of the reward in lines 11. But to adopt this emphasis ignores the much more basic contrast between lines 4-6 and lines 9-11. The contrast asserts an inescapable conflict between the desire for men's honor and the desire for God's praise. To insert the idea of the publicity of God's reward destroys the carefully articulated structure and must therefore postdate it. Whether God's reward is given openly or in secret falls outside the central intention of the three stanzas.

Behind a second textual variant there may lie a theological concern. In A 9 man's action in giving alms takes place in secret—in C 9 man's action is seen by the Father who is in secret; in B 9 the texts vary: many Mss. treat the point in harmony with C 9 (i.e., a man prays to the Father who is in secret), but the Western Mss. treat this as parallel to A 9 (i.e., a man prays in secret). Does the choice of variant here affect the meaning? It does not seem to change the character of the actions, since all three are carried out in ways hidden from other men. Moreover, all clearly imply the omniscience of God. He is one from whom no such secret can be hid. But do B 9 and C 9 intentionally stress the fact that God is in secret? Is it important that he be known as one who dwells in the secret place? (Such a nuance would be quite the reverse of the adverb *openly* in the previous variant.) One may well doubt whether so subtle an intention is needed to explain the origin of these variants. The change may have been occasioned by the different kinds of action in A, B and C 1. Prayer and fasting are actions which are oriented toward God in a way not so true of almsgiving, where one person gives a coin to another. In the two actions which embody penitence before God and dependence on him, the invisibility of God is essential to the action; it does not seem so constitutive of the action of giving alms. Therefore, although we do not wish to stress any special significance in this variant, it is a reminder that man's actions in secret relate him to God's presence in secret, both Father and sons thus sharing in the same kind of hiddenness. The inner reality of one is linked to the inner reality of the other.

There are other points where the Matthean text diverges from the arbitrary and artificial symmetry of our sketch. Frequently the reason for this divergence is recoverable. For instance, in A 4 the motive is a desire to be praised rather than the wish to be seen, as in B 4, C 4. It is the blowing of trumpets which perhaps caused this change, since this image is not so much visible as audible. Again, the variations in lines 8 may be traced to the need for actions precisely the opposite of those in lines 3. The maximum of noise, as made by trumpets, calls for a minimum of sound on the part of the hands. Only in lines 3 and 8 do we find any prolixity of words, and there it is a result of making the hyperboles as vivid as possible. For example, prayers which are freed from the corruption of ostentation must be said not only in one's room, but with the door closed. The one exception that proves this rule is the unnecessary repetition in C 9 of the clause from C 4. This internal resistance to redundancy is witness to the artistry of the construction.

We should now canvass the evidence for accretions during the pre-Matthean stages. Of these at least five may be distinguished with a moderate degree of justification.

> Beware of practicing your piety before men
>   in order to be seen by them;
> for then you will have no reward
>   from your Father who is in heaven.
>
> (*Matt. 6:1.*)

It is doubtful whether this introductory sentence formed part of the original triptych. Several reasons can be cited for this belief. (1) A different verb for *seeing* is adopted. (2) The verse relies wholly on the use of plurals, unlike the three stanzas. (3) The shift from "your (singular) Father who sees in secret" to "your (plural) Father who is in heaven" weakens the thrust of the stanzas in a way which their author would probably not have encouraged. (4) This summary verse is dull and colorless, devoid of vivid aural or visual images, hyperbolic caricatures and satiric deftness. Only an artist could have created the triad, but any pedant could have produced this flat and innocuous prose. (5) The summary is content to stress the negative half of each stanza and fails to cover the positive half which in the original conception of the artist was surely primary. As a result, the introduction distorts the thought of the triptych as a whole, something which its author would be loathe to do.[9] The catechist who added this convenient summary was not concerned with the profound theological and ethical advantages of secrecy, but only with the more obvious dangers of excessive ostentation. His mind was not unlike that of Justin Martyr for whom it was sufficient to preserve this first verse alone (Apol. I, 15, 17). This particular catechist may have wished to introduce only the first of the three stanzas. This is probable if we adopt

[9] Here I side against A. George, "La justice . . . ," p. 592, and with J. O'Hara, "Christian Fasting," pp. 3-4, and R. Bultmann, *The History of the Synoptic Tradition*, p. 150. I am not content, however, with O'Hara's assignment of the verse to the Matthean redactor.

the variant reading which uses almsgiving instead of righteousness or piety (RSV).[10]

Even though we assign the addition of this verse to a pre-Matthean catechist, we absolve him of conscious intent to corrupt the thought of the triad. Pedestrian minds often reduce prophetic hyperbole to perfunctory platitudes without knowing it. Moreover, we note that this catechist did nothing to accentuate the anti-Pharisaic polemic, passing over the more blatant sins of the hypocrites. Perhaps his emendation took place before that warfare reached its height or in circles where it was dormant. Even so, his addition does indeed damage the positive force of lines 8-11 and encourages readers to assume that what follows is nothing but conventional moralizing. His limp conception of the pericope is shared by many recent exegetes.

If the catechist who added vs. 1 intended it to cover all three stanzas, as is likely, then his emendation was probably adopted before the addition of vss. 7-15, for that addition seriously inhibited later teachers from recognizing the integrity of the earlier triptych. This interpolation of eight verses included no fewer than three separate accretions, none of which harmonizes with the intention of the triptych. Each change was accomplished by someone who failed to discern the coherence of the three stanzas.

The earliest of the three was the teaching in vss. 7, 8. Several different forces may have attracted it to this setting. The first is simply the word for praying. In the second stanza (vss. 5, 6) that word appears four times; its appearance in vs. 7 provided a natural link. Moreover in vs. 5 there was a negative command which invited association with the two negative commands of vss. 7, 8. If Christians should not imitate the hypocrites, neither should they imitate the Gentiles. It was the habit of early Christian catechists to define Christian duties by setting them over against both Jew and Gentile practice. That is what has happened here. If Jewish scribes sought the full rewards of publicity, Gentile priests sought

[10] This is a case which W. Nagel thinks should be reopened. Cf. *Vigiliae Christianae* 15 (1961): 141-48.

to impress their gods with verbosity and volume. Probably vss. 7, 8 circulated separately at first, with their contrast between the noisy frenetic jabbering of Gentiles and the quiet, confident, simple petitions of the churches. Then the picture of the contrast between the hypocrisy of synagogue prayers and the hiddenness of private prayers induced a teacher somewhere to conflate these two contrasts, unaware that he was destroying the symmetry of the triad. Both contrasts are valid, of course. They may be of comparable age and authenticity. Yet the intrusion of the second served to hide the earlier balance and to divert attention away from its own proper insight.

Because of this damage, wrought, I think, by the addition of vss. 7, 8, it became easier to increase the separation of stanza two from stanza three by the insertion of the Lord's Prayer. The different location of this prayer in Luke as well as in other early Christian writings indicates that its location in Matthew is also quite adventitious. It bears no logical relation to vs. 6 but illustrates public rather than private praying (e.g., all the pronouns are plural). Its logical relation to vs. 8 is no closer, for its collection of petitions, however simple and direct, is a rather curious illustration of the truth of that verse. Its form reflects frequent repetition (three times according to the Didache) which to some critics is the precise fault of the Gentile praying of vs. 7. Lacking any formal connection to the triptych, lacking as well any logical link to the argument of its context, the Prayer reveals only a verbal and a topical link to this context. This fact, in turn, suggests that this insertion was made by a catechist who was charged with collecting and arranging teachings on the topic of prayer, one whose basic library was provided by oral rather than by written materials.

Before this prayer was attracted to this location, a step which probably had been taken before the Matthean redaction, it already had attracted to itself the supplementary teaching of vss. 14, 15. This teaching lacks any verbal or conceptual link to its sequel in vss. 16 ff., to the first two stanzas in the triad, or to the Gentile practices in vss. 7, 8. The only gravitational impulse was provided by the petition in vs. 12. The Lord's Prayer, unlike the triad, had enough cohesive power to reject the insertion of this saying between vs. 12 and vs. 13. There is also abundant evidence for the separate existence of vss. 14, 15. This makes altogether probable the notion that the combination of vss. 9-13 and 14, 15 had taken place in oral tradition before the merged unit was inserted as a further appendix to the second of our two stanzas.

The study of post-Matthean variants in the text of the Lord's Prayer is an illuminating project in itself, but it has little direct bearing on our exploration of the command to secrecy. Such study would be diversionary in the same way that the three accretions of vss. 7-15 were diversionary in the early church. One may well ponder why successive teachers have encouraged these diversions in defiance of the artistic and theological profundities of the central triad. Surely the diversions give an unwitting witness to the unpopular character of that triad. No religious establishment takes delight in it. No cliques of cultists are encouraged to exploit it. It is not the stuff out of which religious crusades emerge. One could use it as a call to a post-religious form of Christianity, but the triptych would immediately suggest that such a call should be uttered to oneself in his own inner room. It is so superbly constructed as a prophetic demand that it becomes poor material for catechetical indoctrination in conventional institutional practices. It is small wonder that reformers and teachers have found little "practical" use for it. Small wonder, then, that every substantial and successive change in this tradition moves away from any profound comprehension of its earliest core. That, at least, is one conclusion regarding the five stages we have analyzed:

the addition of 6:1 as a summarizing introduction
the inclusion of 6:7, 8 as a supplementary negative foil
the conflation of 6:9-12 with 14-15
the interpolation of that amalgam between 6:8 and 6:16
the textual alteration of 6:4, 6, 18 "openly."

Theological Implications

By setting aside these diversionary accretions and by focusing afresh on the triple demand, we may now be in a position to appraise the character of its author's theology, as well as the theological orientation of the community which heard and preserved it.

What inferences may be drawn concerning the vision of God which is native to the command itself? No doubt is left concerning the desires of that God. He hates hypocrisy and requires of his sons unconditional and uncompromised integrity. He discerns hypocrisy in the deepest roots of man's action, where desires for social recognition have their birth. In this respect God's thoughts are other than men's, for men use their religious and communal desires to reinforce each other, but to him those two desires are utterly incompatible. If a person seeks praise from both men and God, he may succeed in one but he will fail in the other, for God rejects religious prestige and social honor as marks of conformity to his will. So accustomed are men to the pious point of view which is flatly rejected in lines 1-6 that they find a rejection of that point of view incomprehensible. Usually religious men, and not least their leaders, rely upon the existence of a kind of God who enforces the ethos which is rejected here. So this command poses a conflict between two gods, one of whom it declares to be false. False is the god who legislates a set of religious duties, establishes a community to observe them, enables that community to identify its rewards with his, and then encourages individual leaders to seek those rewards as the divinely authorized road to salvation. This triptych rejects every idea of God whose primary approach to men is by way of endorsing patterns of behavior which undergird prevailing social and religious systems. This teaching repudiates all ideas of transcendence which support the kinds of righteousness here labeled hypocrisy, including even some which hail God as Father. By its radical repudiation of most gods, this command discloses what is meant by trust in the gospel (Mark 1:15).

This triptych defines very precisely and very inclusively the nature of hypocrisy, by reference to the relationships pertaining between the Father who sees in secret and his sons whose intentions and actions are in secret. Hypocrites are not his sons; he is not their Father. Men are his sons only when their acts of charity are hidden from themselves (cf. 6:2-4 with Matt. 25:31-46), only when their prayer to him is unpolluted by pretensions to piety, only when their fasting is invisibly inseparable from rejoicing. At the secret place where such integrity emerges one finds both his paternal action and their filial response. This is the place where repentance (e.g., fasting) takes place, or the new creation, or birth as sons of God. That term sons points to the action in which they seek his perfection (Matt. 5:48) and in which they receive his reward. His demand for such an action ("when you give alms, pray, fast, or do anything else") is intrinsic to the ontological nature of both God and men. The secret merging of their action with his illustrates the mysterious interconnections between transcendence and immanence. Any notion of the covenant between Father and sons which encourages the hypocrisy of lines 2 is false theology. It operates wtih an understanding of God's omniscience which is quite different from that embodied in lines 10 and 11. It expects a set of divine rewards (cf. line 3) and thereby reflects false conceptions of the Father's omnipotence. It locates God's primary presence not in man's heart, where the concept of omnipresence belongs, but in the prevailing cultural and religious customs and/or standards of judgment. In short, hypocrites (lines 2) operate with a theology which they deeply believe to be true but which is actually false, that is, if the creator of this triple demand is right.

The hypocrite operates as well with a false anthropology, a false conception of sonship. He is of course unconscious of this, and his careful observance of the demands of righteousness only deepens his unawareness. From this standpoint, religious institutions foster self-deception. Even when those institutions discourage the more obvious kinds of ostentatious piety and ambitious quests for prestige, the desire to be seen by men can subtly insinuate itself into the holiest moment. Moreover, we must recall that the forms of piety pictured in the triptych are intended to suggest many types of human behavior, whether secular or religious. These types may change from culture to culture, from century to century, but desires for social approval remain constant. By attacking those desires at the point of their ultimate theological legitimation, Jesus' demand undermines the mythological sanctions which support all social structures, whether avowedly religious or not.

There is more here, however, than an abstract notion of man and of society. There is a sustained and well-planned strategy to transform men from hypocrites into sons. Who can claim to be free from that form of hypocrisy which is defined here? For those who cannot, the teaching is a call to repentance, a call which opens the way to restoration of the integrity of true selfhood. This call can become a force creative of the new man, whose purity of heart enables him to see in secret the God who also sees in secret. No other reward is needed by his sons than to become his sons (Matt. 5:48). Here again we may see how repentance and trust are conjoined and how man's action indicates the fulness of the time and the approach of God's kingly authority (Mark 1:15).

What may one deduce about Christology from this triptych? First, line 5—"truly I say to you"—is an assertion of authority by a teacher who claims to know whereof he speaks. Also in lines 10, 11—"your Father will reward"—he asserts without qualification his knowledge of God's action. This claim to authority is advanced with the presumed consent of the audience, at least that audience which has endorsed the value of the three stanzas by remembering them. Moreover, we may note that such a teacher must secure this endorsement in ways consistent with the logic of the teaching. Extrinsic social plaudits are ruled out as evidence or proof of his authority. If this teacher had sought to legitimize his status by public actions of charity or fasting, not only would he have contradicted himself, he would have proved himself the greatest hypocrite of all. The only road to legitimacy must be one which respects this "blood test" of paternity. Approached from this angle, the triptych may contribute little to formal theories concerning Christ's being and status, but it helps to exclude many fraudulent types of christological speculation. Christ could command such behavior from his followers, and he could ground that command in an announcement of the good news and in his knowledge of God's will, but he could not vindicate that knowledge by signs which would convince the public of his own piety or power.

Efforts to describe Christ's uniqueness as Son of God should not dissolve the bonds of solidarity either with the Father or with the other sons, bonds which are intrinsic to this triptych. The positive picture of intentional actions in lines 7-11 must be applicable to Jesus himself, or else the whole tradition of the early church would be falsified. The teachings confront us not only with brilliant hyperboles and with penetrating insights into psychological realities, but, to use Father George's telling phrase, with "the law of his life," a law which has been quietly jettisoned by many Christologies.[11] For one whose fasting was so secret as to be hidden by joy and whose prayers were uncorrupted by public performance, his hesitation to flaunt divine authority must have been far more than calculated strategy. It must instead have been in tune with the kind of sonship-in-secret which is articulated in this triptych.

Ecclesiology is determined by Christology. The idea of church must harmonize with the idea of sonship if the church is to be considered a family of sons. Yet, as we have noted, it is the inveterate tendency of religious institutions to use publicity to reward piety, and thus to solicit the kind of hypocrisy condemned by Jesus. No doubt the early church fell afoul of this tendency. Yet it was also the type of community which preserved these anti-establishmentarian rules. The inner actuality of the Christian community must coincide with the inner actuality of the son-Father relationships as commanded here. The church is not truly his church when it encourages the hypocrisy condemned here; it becomes the family of God

[11] A. George, "La justice . . . ," p. 598; cf. Mark 10:18.

only when the cohesion of its inner fabric and its standards of greatness are in harmony with the kind of invisible piety which Jesus commanded.

Does the triptych permit inferences concerning that type of eschatology which is most congenial to it? Not at first sight, for there is no explicit mention of the kingdom of God. Yet if one identifies the expectation of the Kingdom with the issuing of final rewards and punishments, and if one discerns in lines 6 and 11 the finality of judgment announced by him whom Christians accepted as judge, then these stanzas must be analyzed as exercizing an eschatological function. What can be said about that function? There are basically two options.

First, one can read this threat and promise in such a way as to stress the difference between the tenses of the verb: present tense in the threat, future tense in the promise. The Kingdom, where the promise will be fulfilled, is future, wholly future. This option is expressed by the textual variant "he who sees in secret will reward you *openly*." The punishment (A 6) is immediate; the reward (A 11) is delayed until an expected settlement at the final great assize at the end of history.

But there is a second option. The future tense is a way of recognizing that obedience to this command is yet to be secured. Both the action and its recompense are potential only. Moreover, the nexus between man's action and God's reward is too intimate to be separated by a time lag between today and the anticipated eschaton. The Father already sees the secrets of man's heart. There is no time lag in vision. The Kingdom comes where God's will is done (Matt. 6:9); this will is done in the entire sequence of actions: the issuing of the command, its audition, its enactment, and its recompense. The advent of God's rule is as near and as distant as the act of obedience and the granting of the reward. That advent is as mysterious as the dialectic interplay of demand-response-reward, an interplay understood as an actualization of fatherhood and sonship in "the purity of heart which wills one thing." To be sure, such an approach to eschatology does not exhaust its meaning or dispel its mystery, but it provides a beachhead of intelligibility which can be extended after other teachings are consulted.

I am convinced that this second option is the preferable one. If so, we may note an important consequence. Since *option one* would have represented the normal expectations in Jesus' day, Jesus' choice of *option two* means that in this case he was intentionally rejecting the common expectations of the final Judgment Day. He was demythologizing that myth! Moreover, the inner rationale of this new interpretation should be seen to result from his discernment of the ethical crisis which every man faces when he chooses between the subtler forms of hypocrisy and purer forms of piety. He who abandons all other rewards except those given by such a Father will pray to this Father in secret, and in so doing he will encounter One who can discern every duplicity and grant utter sincerity to his sons. The family of sons becomes his new creation, heirs of his Kingdom. Eschatology is demythologized by this action, for the truth of the announcement "The time is fulfilled" is verified in the event of repentance and trust which accompanies the command of Christ.

A Final Question

Some of the foregoing cogitations have been based upon the assumption that the earliest core of this teaching comes to us from Jesus. Is that assumption tenable? The truth of the teachings does not depend on a positive answer, nor does obedience to the demand depend upon any theory of its origin. Yet the question remains legitimate and important. Although the scope of this essay does not permit me to mount a massive defense of Jesus as author, and although I disavow the perspectives of many who try to recover *ipsissima verba Christi,* I can suggest the range of evidence which might be cited.

First of all is the form of the teaching itself. It represents careful construction by a prophetic artist who was a master of hyperbole, of satire, of imagery, and of penetration to the heart of the matter.

Second is the evidence that, before the Matthean edition appeared, the teaching had passed through at least five stages of development. The threefold command should probably be assigned to a period of oral transmission at the very inception of those developments.

Third, there are many features in this construction which reflect a Jewish milieu characteristic of Judea and Galilee before the church had completely broken away from the synagogue. The triptych betrays no trace of Gentile thought or practice, no echo of the death or resurrection of Jesus, none of the prejudices unique to the post-resurrection church.

Fourth, there is a high level of correlation between this teaching and others generally attributed either to Jesus or to the very earliest stages of oral tradition. One finds similar teachings on hypocrisy and on reward, similar demands for the single eye and for total obedience, a similar tendency to make black and white distinctions in moral judgments. The almsgiving requirement coheres with other demands for selling all one's goods in order to give to the poor. Other teachings on prayer stress the same intimate son-father relationships. Only in the case of fasting does there seem to be a lack of supporting evidence. It was widely recognized that Jesus and his disciples did not openly fast; in this they were unlike John's disciples (Matt. 9:14-17; 11:16-19). There is doubt as to how we should construe the explicit teaching in C 1-11. Does this represent a complete repudiation of fasting as an external and visible practice, and an approval of fasting only when it is an inner attitude devoid of any external sign?[12] That is one possible way of viewing the teaching. On the other hand, the teaching may presuppose an approval of synagogue practice and a rejection only of excessive ostentation. "He could scarcely have meant that fasting, as an external exercise of humiliation, . . . has no place in the Christian order of things."[13] Either of these options can draw upon other teachings of Jesus for support. There is some evidence

[12] Cf. T. W. Manson, *The Sayings of Jesus* (London: SCM Press, 1957), p. 172.

[13] J. O'Hara, "Christian Fasting," p. 15.

of his approval of existing institutions and some evidence of repudiation. But to limit the decisions to these two options is probably wrong. "When you fast . . ." remains ambiguous. Probably that is the intention of the triptych. To attribute special virtue either to fasting or to its rejection would contradict the central point of the demand. Whether or not Jesus fasted, and whatever the practices of his disciples and of the earliest church, the thrust of the demand itself stands unchanged. It remains true that among the potential authors of this teaching the most likely source is Jesus himself.

4 Love and Lend

Arduous is this, and wholly opposed to the nature of man; but there is nothing too arduous to be overcome by the power of God.

John Calvin,
Commentary on the Epistle to the Romans

When we organize the teachings of Jesus according to topic or according to the kind of visible action, as is usually done in books on the ethics of Jesus, we see little reason for associating his instructions on fasting with those on charity. Jesus connected what we disjoin. The reasons for this contrast between his practice and ours are worth examining, for such mental habits are often indicative of a fundamental difference in world views. For example, in our previous chapter we have seen how he joined three quite diverse types of action, all illustrating decisive contrasts in the implicit relationship between God and the self. They demonstrated either hypocrisy or freedom from the desire for social status, and they disclosed the roots of action in either the coming kingdom of God or in demonic deceptions; therefore they belonged together.

The same contrast inheres in the classification of the commands which we now examine. Here we treat separately the command on treatment of enemies from that on the lending of money. Jesus seems to have united them. Even more strikingly, where we see no connection between the action of retaliation against evildoers and the mode of praying, Jesus' world view necessarily brought to bear on them the same considerations. Let us then try to locate these connections in the following verses.

A	B	C
1. Love your enemies	1. Do good to those who hate you	1. (Do not refuse him who would borrow from you) (Matt. 5:42b)
2. If you love	2. If you do good to	2. If you lend to
3. those who love you	3. those who do good to you	3. those from whom you hope to receive
4. what credit is that to you?	4. what credit is that to you?	4. what credit is that to you?
5. For even sinners	5. For even sinners	5. Even sinners
6. love those who love them	6. do the same	6. lend to sinners to receive as much again
7. Love your enemies	7. Do good [to those who do evil]	7. Lend, expecting nothing in return

8. And your reward will be great
9. You will be sons of the Most High
10. For he is kind to the ungrateful and the selfish.

(*Luke 6:27, 32-35.*)

If we examine carefully the formal structure of this triptych, we detect features similar to the three stanzas in Matt. 6:2-6, 16-18. A triple command is supported by a triple illustration, three diverse actions (love, doing good, lending) being motivated by a single intention. Not only do the three parallel one another, but each is based upon a striking antithesis. The conditional clause ("If you love . . ." lines 2, 3; cf. "When you fast" of Matt. 6:16) introduces the evil consequence ("sinners," lines 5, 6; cf. "hypocrites" of Matt. 6:2). This evil consequence forfeits any claim on reward from God. Line 4, "What credit is that?" may seem quite different from "They have their reward" in Matt. 6; yet beneath the surface the same logic controls the thought. The question "what credit?" can only be answered by "none at all." Those who give good for good have in fact already received their reward. God's rewards go only to those who have foresworn such a reward from men. The chief formal contrast between the two trilogies is that in this case the three positive promises of reward are telescoped into one (lines 8, 9, 10).

That very fact, however, stresses the congruity not only of these three actions in Luke 6 but of their congruity with the three actions in Matt. 6:2-6, 16-18. All six teachings are definitions of sonship, of fatherhood, of the filial relation. All six focus on the contradiction between rewards from men and from God, and therefore between selfish and unselfish concern. All six determine the character of an action by assessing its total genesis and course: from God's action through man's heart where desire emerges, to the choice of specific modes of action, to the effect on others and the repercussions on the self. When one weighs carefully the congruities in form, function, and rationale, he is bound to conclude that all six commands were shaped in the same laboratory, where they were designed by the same teacher for the same community of people, a people who in their desire to become sons of God have accepted his authority to disclose God's will and way. In his world such sonship provided a single set of criteria for measuring the acceptability of all types of behavior.

There are differences, to be sure, between the prohibition of the hatred of enemies in Luke 6:32 and that of ostentatious almsgiving in Matt. 6:2; but such differences are relatively minor. In the former, for example, men must not imitate the "sinners," while in the latter they must not be like the "hypocrites." But that change is quite intelligible. When a man loves those who love him, the presence of hypocrisy is not so obvious. He may not be trying to deceive others. Nor is he necessarily deceiving himself. It is not clear that he has decided to seek social approval instead of divine reward. Even so, if he limits his love to those who love him, that love is no longer the love of God (line 10), and he becomes a hypocrite by the standards of Matt. 6:2-3. Nevertheless, in the context of Luke 6:32 the concept "sinner" becomes the more natural foil for the appeal. Other teachers, however, evidently thought the term sinners too innocuous or too general. The Matthew version includes two categories especially scorned by pious Jews: publicans and Gentiles (5:46,47). Presumably this would strengthen the negative motivation. The Didache joins Matthew in pilloring the Gentiles (1:3); to Justin Martyr whores better exemplify those who love their lovers, and Gentiles are men who lend in order to receive interest (Apol. I, 15, 9-13). Such minor variations on the theme reflect variations in the Christian environment. They both assume and strengthen popular prejudices; yet, rather curiously, they do so in the interest of the love of enemies. The skeptic may well make something out of the intrinsic contradiction in a teaching which thus employs prejudice against sinners and whores to motivate unprejudiced actions.

Where does the earliest triptych end? With Luke 6:35, or 6:36, or even later? Various answers appear in the tradition. The literary form which we have isolated assists us in selecting those answers which fit most neatly into this particular setting. Line 8, "your reward will be great," appears to be essential in providing the antithesis to line 4, "what credit?" In this regard the Lukan tradition has surely remained closer to the source than has the Matthean, which dropped this item. But can we halt the flow of thought with line 8? Such a terminus is rather difficult to conceive. Rather, line 9, "you will be sons," appears to be a necessary definition of the reward, and that assertion of sonship in turn seems to require as its logical support line 10, "for he is kind." Thus from lines 1 through 10 there is nothing illogical or extraneous. The only asymmetrical element is the brevity of B 7 and the absence in Luke of C 1. There are points in which C 3 and C 6 do not precisely parallel A 3 and A 6, but this variation is the result of differences native to the action of loving and lending. Whereas in the former both parties are in a position to love, in the latter only one party is in a position to lend.

This symmetry was obscured or destroyed in other versions of the teaching. One may, for example, examine the variations in lines 9, 10 where Luke mentions two categories: the ungrateful (ἀχαρίστους—does this category match the χάρις of vs. 32, or refer to borrowers unable to repay?) and evil (πονηρούς—does this cover the first and second of the three groups or only the second?).[1] By contrast Matthew specifies that God is kind to both the evil and the good, the righteous and the unrighteous (5:45). Like Matthew, the Didache stresses God's goodness to all (1:5), and like him the Gospel of the Naassenes balances two pairs, the righteous and the unrighteous, the holy and the sinful. Justin also follows Matthew in stressing God's goodness to both good and evil. Only Luke limits the reference to those who can or will not reciprocate. I believe that Luke has better preserved the point of the teaching, which is not at all concerned with good action toward the good nor with the evenhandedness of God's justice, but only with the profligate generosity of the Father and his sons toward men who can give nothing in return. This does not deny the truth of the sun-and-rain analogy, but it does in fact express a doubt whether that analogy originally accompanied the triple command of Luke 6:32-35.

Did this teaching unit originally end with line 10 (Luke 6:35)? We should reckon with the possibility that a pre-Matthean tradition linked it to the triptych which is now found in Matt. 6:2-6, 16-18. I have already stressed the basic congeniality of these two units. It is nonetheless probable that the two did not originate on the same occasion. We should also reckon with the possibility that a pre-Lukan tradition associated the triptych with Luke 6:36 and with the commands of Luke 6:37, 38. Here the continuities both in modes of action and motivation are strong indeed. "Be merciful" condenses into one the three commands of vs. 35*a;* "as your Father is merciful" is simply an alternate way of putting vs. 35*b*. Thus in content, though not in form, vs. 36 is an appropriate conclusion to the preceding unit. (Surely the Lukan concept of mercy is more congenial than the Matthean notion of perfection, Matt. 5:48.) But vs. 36 is also excellent intro-

[1] The symmetry of the pericope would be enhanced if we emended line 10 to include three categories—ἐχθρούς, πονηρούς, and ἀχαρίστους.

duction to the four commands which follow. "Be merciful" is there defined by four actions: "judge not, condemn not, forgive, give." The four commands are obviously in line with the three commands of vs. 35 and the single command of vs. 36.

However, a new structure and rhythm have been introduced which bespeaks origin on a different occasion. In this case the patterns are twofold and fourfold. Each command is followed immediately by a promise which repeats the same verb; two negatives are followed by two positives. The formal symmetry is almost perfect.

Judge not	and you will not be judged
Condemn not	and you will not be condemned
Forgive	and you will be forgiven
Give	and it will be given you.

The reasoning is precisely the same as in the preceding triptych. To be sure, in that teaching the rewards from men were explicitly set over against the reward from God. Yet the same contrast is implicit here. These four commands make sense only if the four promises ("you will not be judged," etc.) refer to God's action. Moreover, each of the four commands represents implicitly a canceling of the expectation of reciprocity from men. The quatrain is as radical as the triptych in setting an absolute opposition between compensations from men and from God, and in requiring of God's sons actions wholly akin to God's uncalculating generosity.

The same reasoning permeates the quatrain which we found in the triptych in Luke 6:32-35, and the triptych in Matt. 6:2-6, 16-18. Yet by reason of contrasts in form we have assigned them to different occasions and origins. That fact makes their congruence of thought all the more impressive. Moreover, this congruence is now seen to apply to a widening range of actions—three in Matt. 6, three in Luke 6:35, four in Luke 6:37, 38. To be sure, there is considerable overlapping: the giving in Luke 6:38 may repeat the same command in Luke 6:35 and in Matt. 6:2. Nevertheless the same principle is capable of indefinite extension. This is suggested by the axiom in Luke 6:38*c*, "The measure you give will be the measure you get back." This axiom could, of course, mark the triumph of a narrow legalistic tit-for-tat ethic. But not in this context, for the decisive measure clearly refers to the superabundance of God's gifts (vs. 38*b*), and it is this superabundance that becomes the ground for his commands. As Luke has arranged these teachings, therefore (probably following a pre-Lukan edition), the underlying motif, from as early as the beatitudes of 6:20-21, is the contrast between actions accompanied by human rewards and those receiving God's blessing. When the reader allows himself to follow the trajectory of this conviction beyond vs. 38 he may well discern a new thrust in the parable of blind leaders (vs. 39). A disciple becomes a blind leader if he adopts a contrary conviction. The mercy of God which has become the basis of Jesus' vocation must become the basis for the disciple as well (vs. 40). Otherwise his condemnation of a brother (vs. 41) in defiance of the commands of Luke 6:27, 35, 37, etc. automatically makes him a hypocrite, his sight impeded by a huge log. This same logic pervades the following parables as well—the tree, the treasures of the heart, the building of the house. This gives ample justification for believing that in his editing work, Luke maintained the basic integrity and radicalism of Jesus' insight into the ways of God and the hearts of men.

This is not to deny to Luke a real degree of editorial freedom to change the traditions as they came to him. For example, I doubt if his version of the Golden Rule originally belonged here. One can of course see how it may have drifted into this pocket. Its definition of *what* a person should do toward others may accord with the other commands. But its conception of *why* contradicts the answers in 6:35, 36 and elsewhere. It accepts human reactions as a measure of one's actions, and does not reflect the contrast in adjacent verses between God's rewards and man's or between selfish and unselfish motivations. It does not really deserve the popular caption *Golden Rule*, for it can conceivably be obeyed by men to whom Jesus says, "What credit is that to you?"

Again, Luke may have been responsible in vss. 27, 28 for replacing the three commands of vs. 35 (which seem to be required by the trilogy in vss. 32-34) by four commands, although these four convey precisely the same common denominator of meaning as the three:

> Love your enemies
> Do good to those who hate you
> Bless those who curse you
> Pray for those who abuse you.

The Greek form is even more symmetrical than the English. First comes the verb in the second person plural followed by plurals of the recipients of the action. The four descriptions of those recipients suggest that the recipients in each case are in the wrong. This gives to the four commands a degree of unity as four definitions of love, to be carried out by a single community of disciples toward a single set of antagonists. In the Greek there is a high degree of assonance at the beginning and end of each line. The quatrain is smoothly shaped to facilitate memorization for quick reference.

It may or may not have originated in conjunction with the following quatrain which has a different form and syntax and visualizes much more specific and individualized situations. Yet the symmetry is equally noteworthy:

> To him who strikes you [singular] on the cheek,
> offer the other also.
> From him who takes away your cloak,
> do not withhold your coat as well.
> To everyone who begs,
> give.
> From him who takes your goods,
> do not ask for them back.

The clause "to him" alternates with the clause "from him"; positive commands, "give," alternate with prohibitions, "do not ask." Much more sharply than in the Golden Rule is there an intended imbalance between action and reaction; the action is the opposite of the reaction. Moreover, the inclusion of the command to give shows that this teaching is not limited to one group—to enemies. The precarious existence of the Christian community may have led to an accent upon how to meet violent efforts to destroy it, but the teaching on giving (cf. Matt. 6:2; Luke 6:34, 35) exhibits a broader horizon.

Our survey of the commands to love and to lend has thus far been quite extensive in turning up many units, in diverse forms, each with a separate history. Yet we have virtually limited our survey to some twenty verses in Luke. So widespread was the circulation of these and cognate commands that a full survey of the parallel forms and successive stages would require many volumes. Surely the saying attributed to Jesus in Acts 20:35 belonged within this same orbit of thought: "It is more blessed to give than to receive," although it is impossible to establish direct links. In later versions one can at times discern the introduction of alien considerations. Two examples from many may suffice.

> Love those who hate you *and you will have no enemy.*
> (*Didache 1:3.*)

That assurance has no place in the triptych with which we began; it employs, in fact, a quite contrary kind of motivation. The primary reference to God's mercy has been displaced by the reference to man's response.

> If anyone would take your goods, do not ask them back,
> For you are not able. (*Didache 1:4.*)

Sometimes the addition of such a clause clearly destroys the symmetry of both form and thought. Sometimes, of course, a later editor may improve upon the balance. For example, the version in Justin Martyr (Apol. 1.15.10) brings together more natural opposites than either Luke or Matthew.

> Love those who hate you.

Instead of tracing the dozens of variants in second-century traditions, however, we shall concentrate on the more familiar version in Matt. 5. There we find two blocs: one series of six commands (vss. 39-42) and another series of two (vs. 44).

The series of six is introduced by the command "Do not resist one who is evil." That introductory command serves a double function. It seems intended as a summary of the other five. This summary, in turn, provides a contrast to the law concerning an eye for an eye. Both functions are quite dubious, and we suspect that the command not to resist evil has been devised by the editor. It is a poor summary because one commandment is not covered: "Give to him who begs from you." The beggar is not necessarily an evil man, and this command is therefore not an instance of non-retaliation. Moreover, none of the others illustrates the passive principle of not resisting an evil man; rather, they command positive actions which double the damage done by him—two cheeks for one, or two miles for one. In effect, then, this command reduces the range and rigor of the others. Why, then, was such a poor summary chosen? Perhaps because it provided a contrast with the scriptural law. The effect of this is to modify the motivation of the other commands. In the Lukan version, as well as in Matt. 5:45, the commands are based on the contrast between those who are sons of God and those who are not. By extending unrecompensed generosity, men can exhibit the Father's mercy. This idea had nothing directly to do with the conflict between the new law and the old, or with proving the superiority of Jesus and his disciples over their Jewish predecessors. The orientation of the pre-Matthean collection was probably quite different from the Matthean version, since the common denominator of the six is not to be found in their relation to the Law.

Similar alterations can be located in the series of two demands in 5:44. The desire to show the contrast to the old law has induced an editor, perhaps Matthew, to create the commandment to hate the enemy, for it is impossible to find such a provision in the Jewish law. This antithesis also deflects attention from the real reason for the two commands of vs. 44, presumably because of the desire to prove that Jesus' righteousness was superior to that of the scribes and Pharisees (5:20) as well as the publicans and Gentiles (5:46, 47). Possibly the Matthean version of the last command—"Be perfect" —was a corresponding way of exalting the superiority of the Christian way over both Jews and Gentiles, and also a way of summarizing all the teachings between 5:17 and 5:48. Even though this tends to obscure the central stress on unreciprocated mercy as the mark of sonship, it must be said that Matthew did not delete that stress. He preserves seven commands which visualize seven situations in all of which men are able to become sons of God. The range of situations includes requisitions by soldiers in an occupation army, cruel intentional insults, spontaneous acts of violence, unjustified law suits, acts of robbery, the pleas of beggars, requests for loans, persecution by synagogue leaders. Such actions give the opportunity of sacrificing self-interest as the mark of sonship, and as illustrations and channels of God's mercy. Just as the three illustrations of secret piety in Matt. 6 represent all forms of piety, so these seven illustrations of public behavior represent all forms of societal action. Whatever the form of behavior, the alternatives remained very much the same: to belong to the rich who already have their reward, or to the poor whose stake in the kingdom of God makes them blessed (Luke 6:20-26).

We may now take stock of our progress toward the central aims of the study:

1. This kind of action is recognizable as a form of self-humiliation which helps to define the repentance demanded by Jesus (Mark 1:15).

2. Men were hardly willing to surrender their very tangible claims for justice among men in exchange for the very intangible assurance of rewards from God unless they accepted and trusted the proclamation concerning the Kingdom.

3. The rejection of the usual social patterns of securing equity is nothing less than absolute; this suggests that obedience would be justified only if in fact it can be said that "the time is fulfilled."

4. The teaching forces a person to ask whether God is, after all, so merciful as this, and whether his mercy is as near and as dependable as it must be if "the kingdom of God is at hand."

5. The whole structure of presuppositions and claims—the unstinted generosity of God, the mode of becoming his sons, the dependability of his promises, the validity of his command, the austerity of his enforcement—becomes a matter of the credibility of this particular prophet.

6. That credibility in a case such as this could be tested only by obedience to his commands and could be fully vindicated only within a community where mutual experiences could be shared.

When we probe behind the surface of these commands, we become dimly aware that they are as native to one world view as they are alien to other perspectives. They are corollaries of a distinctive theology, eschatology, anthropology, Christology, and ecclesiology. Surely the ethical substance of the commands is important, but even more important are their far-reaching implications.

Do they dependably echo the message of Jesus? Among the Apostolic Fathers no teaching is more frequently cited than this, and none is considered more distinctive of the Christian pattern of living.[2] In the Didache, this is the substance of the first commandment; Justin points to it as the new discovery in the gospel (Apol.15.9.10). Within the New Testament itself, every major literary tradition gives a prominent place to the demand for the love of enemies. In view of this unanimity it seems safe to say that to doubt that Jesus is the source of this demand would cast real doubt on the doubter's objectivity.

Earlier we referred to the insistence of Professor Norman Perrin that the burden of proof rests on anyone who claims that a particular teaching comes from Jesus. In this instance

[2] Polycarp, Phil. 12:3; Gospel of Thomas 95; II Clement 13:4; W. Bauer, "Das Gebot der Feindesliebe und die Alten Christen," *Zeitschrift für Theologie und Kirche* 27 (1917): 37-54; H. Köster, *Synoptische Überlieferung bei den Apostolischen Vätern* (Berlin: Akademie-Verlag, 1957), p. 44.

Prof. Perrin advances that very claim: "That Jesus challenged his followers in these terms is not to be doubted, and indeed, is never doubted." [3] As a matter of fact, so sure is he of these commands that he does not even try to prove them. I am quite ready to condone his inconsistency in not providing the proof which he has required of others. All of us are adept at requiring others to prove points which we dislike, while avoiding the same tests of our own position. But I am bound to criticize Perrin on other matters. For one thing, I plead a gross disproportion which is characteristic of much current scholarship. In a book entitled "Rediscovering the Teaching of Jesus," the dominant theme is the impossibility of realizing such an objective. Yet when, as in this case, he does rediscover a particular set of commands, he dismisses them with a discussion limited to three pages. Whole chapters are devoted to the case for a radical skepticism, but when the author is forced to surrender that skepticism, he has almost nothing more to say. A second point is the absence of sustained effort to press behind the behavior ordered to the implicit thought-world within which it belongs. To be sure, Perrin mentions the love of God experienced in the forgiveness of sins and in the table fellowship of the Kingdom (p. 148). But these features escape any further scrutiny. How else can we rediscover Jesus' teachings except by pressing beneath their surface to the insights embedded within them? A third point is Perrin's way of dealing with the commands themselves. He rightly sees them as addressed to disciples. But he limits the category "enemies" to men who are gathered around the same table, "a returned prodigal" perhaps. "The challenge is to exceed the normal and natural attitudes of love, affection, kindness and courtesy." Such an interpretation shrinks both the danger and the difficulty and, thereby, the significance of the command. When Perrin visualizes the behavior of disciples away from that table fellowship, he can without any apparent hesitation write of Matt. 5:39*b*-41: "The teaching of Jesus is spectacularly devoid of specific commandments

[3] Norman E. Perrin, *Rediscovering the Teaching of Jesus,* p. 148.

and nowhere is that more evident than in these three sayings. . . . They were never meant to be taken literally. . . . The coat/cloak saying is, literally taken, ridiculous. . . . [These sayings] are quite impossible to carry out except under special conditions and in very limited circumstances."[4]

Accepting with this scholar the authenticity of these commands, I want to urge three obligations on the part of every student: he should apply a greater proportion of his time and energy to the analysis and exegesis of commands like these, he should seek to recover the worldscape of Jesus within which such commands seemed to him to be both natural and necessary, and he should be provoked to assess the distance between that world disclosed in such commands (the kingdom of God) and the world in which our own thinking normally proceeds.

The deepest issue posed by this teaching is not the choice between resistance and nonresistance or between violence and nonviolence or even between loving and hating enemies. The ultimate issue is the choice between two perceptions of reality, two worldscapes, two motivational and reward systems. Perhaps by taking up other difficult but authentic demands, our next chapter will carry us further in the exploration of this issue.

[4] *Ibid.*, p. 147.

5 Become Last of All

The Son of God humbled himself
for you—could you be proud?
The Son of God took the form of
a servant—could you seek to rule?
He became poor—could you run
after riches?
He accepted dishonor—could you
strive after honors?

St. Tykhon, as cited by N. Gorodetzky,
The Humiliated Christ in
Modern Russian Thought

In this essay we turn to a teaching which appears in at least three versions and in at least eight passages in the Synoptic Gospels. Such profusion alerts us to its potential importance both in the outlook of the early church and in the traditions attributed to Jesus. Each of the three versions is based on an unqualified contrast between extreme alternatives stated with maximum brevity and simplicity.

> Whoever exalts himself will be humbled,
> Whoever humbles himself will be exalted.
> (*Matt. 23:12; Luke 14:11; 18:14.*)
>
> The last will be first, and the first last.
> (*Matt. 20:16; Mark 10:31; Luke 13:30.*)
>
> If any one would be first, he must be last of all.
> (*Mark 9:35; Matt. 20:27.*)

Viewed strictly in terms of syntactical structure, none of these represents an actual command. All are assertions, not injunctions. But the assertions are obviously intended to exert pressure on the will of the recipients with a view to altering their conduct in line with the principle. There is imperatival force in the sayings and in each of the contexts. We will select the saying as it appears in Mark 9:35 and observe clues to its earlier and later stages.[1]

The Earlier Strata

We begin with an analysis of the surface stratum. What is the form and function of this proverb in the immediate Markan context?

> And they came to Capernaum; and when he was in the house he asked them, "What were you discussing on the way?" But they were silent; for on the way they had discussed with one another who was the greatest. And he sat down and called the twelve; and he said to them, "If any one would be first, he must be the last of all and servant of all." (*Mark 9:33-35.*)

Anticipating later findings, we shall label this stratum number three. In form, this unit is a tiny paradigm, to use Dibelius' categories, which accents a pithy pronouncement of Jesus, and which provides a sufficiently explicit narrative setting to interpret that pronouncement. This setting is a dispute for primacy among the disciples. Although this dispute is alleged to have arisen during the ministry of Jesus, the story is preserved and is used by Mark because of its continuing relevance to the church in Mark's day. His Gospel offers ample evidence of jealousy and friction among Christian leaders, occasioned by desires for status and preference. Attached to this setting the proverb becomes a trenchant rebuke to quarreling leaders. Although the terms of the axiom are inclusive ("If any one . . .") the paradigm applies in a restricted way to the Twelve in their relations to one another. The function is ecclesiastical rather than catechetical,

[1] Here I follow the substance of my essay "The Morphology of a Proverb," *Anglican Theological Review* 21 (1939) : 282-92.

designed to improve church discipline rather than to proclaim the nearness of the Kingdom.

Within the complete span of Mark's editorial purposes, however, other motifs may have been present in his use of the paradigm. He may have wished, as R. H. Lightfoot suggested, to underscore the blindness of the original disciples in their failure to understand the gospel.[2] He may have been defending the authority of Paul against opponents who were promulgating the superior claims of Peter and the Twelve. Or, struggling with the dilemmas of a Roman church which was being demoralized by violent persecution and by cowardice on the part of its leaders, Mark may have been appealing to those leaders to accept that lowest of all positions —death as martyrs—as their road to greatness. Still another option is to treat the whole of the Gospel of Mark as an account of the training of the Twelve to become the leaders of the crowds of followers (the term disciples in Mark has this limited reference). In this case, the distinctive Markan nuances are conveyed in the shift of locale from the *way* to the *house,* and then back again. These had become highly symbolic terms. The aptness of the paradigm for this purpose has been suggested by its later frequent use in ordination sermons. Yet even though Mark may well have adapted the paradigm for special uses, it is extremely doubtful whether he created the proverb itself.

Is there evidence of earlier strata that enables us to dig beneath this simple paradigmatic stage? A paradigm may originate in various ways: as an authentic reminiscence of a scene in the life of Jesus, as the transformation of a parable or miracle, as the crystallization of church controversies, as the addition of a narrative setting to a floating proverb. To help one choose the more probable alternative, the following questions are relevant. Is the narrative necessary to make the saying intelligible? Are the setting and the saying independent or interdependent? Is there evidence of an earlier separation of the two? Does the same saying appear in other contexts

[2] R. H. Lightfoot, *The Gospel Message of St. Mark* (New York: Oxford Oxford University Press, 1950), pp. 110-16.

and forms? If so, which form best explains the origin of the others?

A cautious application of these tests enables us to find considerable evidence of an earlier form. A glance at the cross-references indicates that the same teaching appears in a variety of forms: paraenesis, legend, symbolical narratives, and isolated proverb. Obviously not all these forms can be primary. A priori, when the same saying appears both as a proverb and as the climax of a paradigm, two possibilities are open: the narrative setting has been supplied to furnish a specific application to the proverb, or an earlier narrative setting has been separated from the proverb. Here we must adopt the former alternative. There is no necessary connection between the proverb and its setting; the context adds nothing that could not be inferred from the content of the proverb itself. The saying has rich meaning apart from the context; in fact, the setting limits its meaning. Moreover, embedded in the Markan paradigm is literary evidence of an original independence. The awkwardness of sequence should be obvious, since between the narrative setting and the climactic saying comes a quite irrelevant clause—"And he sat down and called the twelve; and he said to them . . ." (vs. 35*a*). Why call them together when they are already in the house? Why mention the Twelve when the previous setting had mentioned a rendezvous with them? Why picture Jesus as sitting down in order to teach a single axiom? This puzzle can best be solved by the hypothesis that these words constitute an introduction to a pre-Markan collection of teachings. This same use as an introductory formula appears elsewhere (Mark 4:1, 10; 12:41; 13:3; Matt. 5:1; Luke 4:20; 5:3; John 6:3). In such an introduction, the reference to the teacher's being seated and to his call of the Twelve is both normal and natural. It is easier to explain the addition of the previous narrative than to explain the insertion of this formula in the heart of a paradigm. We are probably dealing, then, with a pre-Markan catena of sayings which had been introduced by 9:35*a* and which continued, with relatively few literary alterations, through 9:50. We may then label this bloc of sayings as stratum two.

In this bloc we note these characteristics: the absence of paradigmatic or biographical narratives to provide exegetical contexts for the sayings; the logical heterogeneity of the sayings; the presence of common words or phrases which provide links of sound rather than sense between adjoining sayings (e.g., "in my name," "offend," "fire," "salt"). These mnemonic aids scattered through the cycle as links in the chain of proverbs indicate the *pre-Markan existence of a "community catechism"* (Bultmann). Thus in stage two of its development our unit was a proverb deposited in a series of pithy axioms which had been arranged for catechetical purposes of the Christian community. The motive seems to have been that of encouraging hospitality and fellowship among Christian leaders and willingness to sacrifice for the common cause. Every leader must be eager to receive others, to be supremely concerned for their salvation, to be ready to be "salted by the fire of persecution," and thus to treat himself as last of all and servant of all. At least ten originally separate sayings have found lodging within this cycle.

Can we penetrate to an earlier nucleus? Surely this catena of axioms in Mark 9:35-50 can hardly be defended as preserving the original order and content. It is difficult to imagine Jesus giving instruction in this manner. The order and arrangement must be artificial, being dependent upon catchwords which aid the memory but do not contribute to smooth-flowing intelligent discourse. The sequence is neither chronological nor logical, but catechetical. We may therefore conjecture an earlier period in which these proverbs circulated separately in oral tradition without biographical setting or pedagogical arrangements. This conclusion is supported by the existence of the same proverb in other cycles of axioms as well as in isolated form; the conclusion becomes almost certain when we notice that cognate forms of the same proverb also circulated separately, attracting specific settings only gradually. An earlier form of the unit, then, is that of a single proverb circulating separately. Can we recover its use and interpretation during this earliest period, which we may label stratum one?

To answer this question we must use data beyond the proverb itself. We must study cognate forms to see if there is a common denominator of meaning and then relate that meaning to what we know of the basic message of Jesus and the earliest church.

One such cognate form is this: "The last shall be first and the first last." This paradox appears in three different contexts: as an interpretation of the parable of the laborers (Matt. 20:16), as a conclusion to the promise of rewards to Jesus' disciples (Mark 10:31), and as strengthening the threat of exclusion from the Kingdom (Luke 13:30). In these passages the interpretation of the same axiom varies according to motive and situation, showing a fluidity of use without fundamental change in the formula itself. An example of this fluidity is provided by the double use in Matt. 19:30 and 20:16, where the Evangelist may have consciously reversed the thrust of the axiom. In 19:30 the accent falls on the promise "the last shall be first," since here the Lord is encouraging the Twelve to make a total sacrifice, i.e., to become last. But in 20:16 the accent falls on the threat, "the first shall become last," because the danger here is that the Twelve (or their successors) might imperil their position by counting on their seniority in leadership to give them privileges superior to those of latecomers.

Then there are sayings which adopt another set of polar terms.

> Whosoever shall exalt himself shall be humbled
> and whosoever shall humble himself shall be exalted.

This saying also appears in three connections: it is conflated with the proverb of Mark 9:35*b* in the extended paraenetic discourse of Matt. 23:11, 12, and it is used to clinch the meaning of two Lukan parables: the choosing of seats (14:11), and the Pharisee and the publican (18:14). Instructive parallels may also be found in the calls to repentance and the demands for childlike humility as prerequisite to Kingdom entrance

(Mark 10:15; Matt. 18:3; John 3:3-5). In inner meaning the proverbs are akin to the Lukan beatitudes and woes, which treat separately the destinies of the "last" and the "first," in accord with the motifs discussed in our previous chapter.

These parallels clarify the probable meaning of the proverb as a primitive axiom. Here we have to do neither with contests for positions of leadership nor with the instruction of converts, but with the prophetic announcement of the Kingdom, with its promise to the lowly meek and its warning to the mighty wicked, addressed to the Jewish community without regard to membership in the church. The proverb in this earliest stage is an axiomatic condensation of Jesus' preaching of the Kingdom, an "authentic echo" of his denunciation of the pride of those who are first and his consolation of those who are last, his demand for repentance (Mark 1:15) and for the surrender of social rights in the name of God's righteousness.

As such, the proverb reflects that revolution in standards of value and in calculations of social status which were produced only by a radically eschatological perspective. The status of being lowliest and least is society's award; the status of becoming greatest and first is God's judgment. The juxtaposition of the two scales of evaluation constitutes the meeting of the old age and the new, the approach of the kingdom of God. Moreover one should not overlook the congeniality of this perspective to that of Luke 6:32-35 and Matt. 6:1-6, 16-18. To be first in the social scale is to receive one's reward now through the operation of human justice ("What credit is that to you?" "You have your reward"). To be last, i.e., to seek no just compensation from men, is to become sons of God and participate in his mercy. There can be no more vicious, subtle, or effective attack on any Establishment than that which is mounted by such aphorisms, since an essential feature in the stability of every social institution is consistency and dependability in the awarding of praise and blame, in the treatment of friends and enemies, in the regulation of credit, and in the recognition of greatness. These proverbs assert a final and permanent rejection of all these necessities.

The Later Strata

This rejection does not wholly disappear in stratum four, as represented by Matt. 18:1-5, but there are substantial modifications. A number of the axioms and one of the paradigms in the Markan cycle have dropped out of this context, presumably because of their fragmentary and disjoined character. The remaining sayings are much more contiguous and consistent in their concern for "the least of these who believe in me" (vs. 6). The series receives an impressive conclusion in a parable transferred from another site (vss. 10-14). The central concern now is the problem of governance within the church. In this edition the disciples are not caught out by their Lord in unholy jealousies; rather, they themselves raise the question, presumably because their later role as rulers and teachers in the churches will require them to know the answer, for they will be in a position to determine preferment and privilege within the church. By what standards will they fulfill this responsibility? It is their duty to their constituency which is set forth by this collection of teachings on humility. As a result, two separate settings (the Markan dispute and the placement of the child) have become one; two separate sayings (Mark 9:35, 37) have been combined to provide a single answer to the initial question. Oral tradition with its rough transitions has become smoothed out into a literary paraenesis with a topical arrangement of standardized teachings. The basic concern has become ecclesiastical (the relation of Christians to one another) and hierarchical (attitudes of leaders toward laymen). The church and Kingdom have tended to coalesce as the radical prophetic challenge has become codified into patterns of established communal behavior. This did not, however, produce a perversion of the initial idea, inasmuch as the leaders are still compelled to subordinate their self-interest to the needs of the "little ones." Greatness in the Kingdom still requires self-humiliation (18:4). The setting has changed, but not the standard.

Luke's use of the Markan story may be labeled stratum five

(Luke 9:46-48). Some changes affect the form, others the interpretation. Like Matthew, Luke has destroyed the simple isolated paradigms by conflating both settings and teachings. He has also omitted several of the disconnected aphorisms, so that the ten or more units of oral tradition become no more than two units of literary tradition, each with its discrete setting. Even greater changes appear in the interpretation, however, and these result chiefly from the changed location of these two units. In Luke they come immediately after a prediction of the suffering of the Son of man, and immediately before the dramatic decision to go to Jerusalem. This location indicates that Jesus himself is the least among them. The proverb thus becomes part of the dramatic record of the rejection of Jesus, giving a harsh specificity to the definition of greatness. In his descent toward death, Jesus is great. A secondary effect is this: anyone who is received in the name of Jesus, however lowly and insignificant he may be or however nonaligned to the disciplic band, confers on his host the same greatness as if he were host to Jesus. Jesus' lowliness/greatness is thus transferable both to "children" and to their hosts. Humility conceived in such terms rebukes the disciples not only for their personal ambition (vs. 46) but for their sectarian exclusiveness as well (vs. 49). In short, Luke gives us more than an abstract teaching on the necessity of becoming last; he presents a vivid contrast between the self-centeredness of the disciples (vss. 45, 46, 49, 54) and the movement toward death on the part of their leader. Greatness is defined simultaneously as servanthood and hospitality.

In stratum six, the use of the axiom in Mark 10:35-45, we may discern even greater changes. The evidence justifies the hypothesis that this longer pericope is a later elaboration of the earlier form as found in Mark 9:33-50. In the later passage (Mark 10:35-45) we find two elements of novelty which have been widely recognized as secondary additions. The reference to the cup which James and John are to share with Jesus is extraneous and late, as is also the appeal to the death of Jesus in vs. 45. If these two elements, recognized on other grounds as intrusions, be removed, we have consistent and unified narrative related at every point to the earlier form of the paradigm in Mark 9. The essentials remain the same; the desire of certain disciples to be first, the resulting dispute, the calling of the twelve to Jesus, the climaxing conclusion as to the true road to greatness.

Each case of sharpened detail in the later account is intelligible as a natural expansion of the earlier anecdote. The setting becomes more circumstantial and personal with the naming of the formerly anonymous disciples. Their petition is made more explicit and concrete and, because there are two questioners, two positions of prestige are described. Their question implies that the disciples already expect both his humiliation and his *second* coming as Messiah, a clear impress of the early church perspective. The teaching is heightened by the use of Gentile rulers as the antithesis to Christian standards. Since both the first and the greatest are mentioned in the teaching, a correspondingly double description of pagan leaders has developed. Finally, the best example of Jesus' teaching is seen to be the death of Jesus himself. To sum up the developments in stage six, we find that the simple unadorned paradigm has been elaborated in many directions. The setting has grown in length and importance until the story of James and John competes for interest with the saying of Jesus; the two chief characters are depicted in such a way as to reflect growing legendary interest in the apostolic martyrs; the nuclear saying is implemented by a new illustration of the vice deplored and by a vivid exemplification of the virtue extolled. We can observe here the process by which a paradigm was transformed into a highly colored legend. In this transformation many motifs are operative: hagiographical, martyrological, apologetic, ecclesiastical, sacramental and christological. These motifs in turn are the expression of a vast range of needs that have emerged from an even broader range of situations in the life of the church. The pericope still preserves the pointed pronouncement of Jesus, but it has now become a prism refracting a broad spectrum of Christian faith and practice.

Multiple motifs may also be discovered in stratum seven,

as presented in Luke 22:24-27. This rendition marks a distinctive application of the anecdote to serve new purposes. The incident is made a part of the Passover meal. In form, the proverb becomes part of the table talk of which Luke is fond.[3] In immediate application, the teaching of humility is defined as table service, an early Christian virtue in which Luke delighted. In its deeper meaning, however, it becomes permeated with the soteriological significance of the Passover and the Passion. "I am in the midst of you as he who serves." The service of Jesus includes both his waiting on them and his atoning death. In fulfilling this function Jesus dramatizes the contrast between his road to greatness and that of the Gentile "benefactors." The guilt of ambition is no longer imputed to James and John, but instead they are assured of salvation and thrones in the Kingdom. In this stage, then, the hagiographical and pedagogical motifs of the Markan pericope recede and new emphasis is given to the sacramental, soteriological, and christological motifs. The atoning death of Jesus has now become the primary context of the proverb. Absent from the early stages in the proverb's history, it is adumbrated in Luke 9:48, becomes explicit in the teachings of Jesus in Mark 10:45, receives symbolic representation in Luke 22:27, and is completely embodied in mythological discourse in stage eight, John 13:3-17.

Turning to this final New Testament step in the proverb's history, we notice profound modifications. In the Lukan pericope the proverb itself is preserved, though attention is focused rather upon the sacramental act of Jesus than upon his teaching. In John the mystical and mythological interpretation of that act makes verbal repetition of the axiom unnecessary, and it disappears. The Lukan symbol provides the transition from the Markan legend to the Johannine myth. In John the primary value does not reside in the teaching of Jesus concerning the reception of the man with the lowest status, nor in his explanation of the road to greatness within the church, as he himself is incontestibly the greatest among

[3] Cf. below, pp. 179 ff.

them, being their Lord (John 13:16). Rather it lies in the abiding service which Jesus continues to render his followers in cleansing them of sins. "If I do not wash you, you have no part in me" (vs. 8). The pericope becomes a profound drama of the timeless operation of divine grace through the presence of the incarnate and atoning Lord.

The career of the proverb can thus be traced from a very early period in the rise of the Christian community to a very late period in which the proverb itself is submerged and its meaning absorbed within the ecclesiastical, sacramental, and mystical experience of that community. Beginning as a pungent threat-promise of an apocalyptic prophet, remembered and repeated by his apostles as an axiomatic condensation of his message, incorporated with similar axioms into the catechetical materials of the emerging churches, attracting to itself narrative contexts that provided specific reference to the problems of discipleship and leadership in those churches, then adapted to the varied purposes of Christian editors, expanding first into a personal legend and then into a sacramental symbol, the axiom finally becomes embodied in an extensive myth of divine grace, a myth that has already been demythologized by the action of Jesus in dying for men. In its life history both the conserving and creating tendencies in gospel tradition are illustrated; the character of the primitive nucleus is recovered and the character of later elaborations illuminated. The oral and literary forms can be distinguished without being made into arbitrary and rigid patterns into which the living tradition must be forced. Rather, the forms are seen as fluid categories responding sensitively to the multiple needs and changing situations of Christian men and women. Each successive stratum illustrates a way in which the message of the earliest Gospel was creatively preserved and colorfully refracted through the prisms of Christian experience. Although the nuclear saying can be defended as being much earlier than Mark and Q, that is not the most important point. For the primitiveness of the gospel tradition is not to be defined simply in terms of its existence in final form at any one moment of time. The units of the tradition do not have existence; they have history. In fact, they *are* their history. And their validity must be defined in terms of the degree to which the history of each unit enshrines the authentic genius of the Christian faith. The history of the tradition interpenetrates the history of the church, and its validity rests upon the continuing validity of the Christian faith and life.

We have no doubt oversimplified the history of the proverb by confining our attention to passages where it is recognizably present. Actually, if we had followed the traces of several cognate themes, a more complex history would have emerged. There are those passages, for example, which stress the necessity of repentance, humility, childlikeness, servanthood. There are numerous pictures of the physician healing the sick rather than the well, the shepherd searching out lost sheep, the prophet feasting with whores and traitors, the exorcist freeing the unclean and the demon-ridden. There are numerous apostolic discussions of the wisdom of God in electing the foolish and the power of God in exalting the weak, illustrations of the saying in the Epistle of Barnabas 6:13, "The Lord saith, 'Behold, I make the last things as the first.' " In short, there is massive documentation for the thesis that the imperative of becoming last summarized the total duty and destiny of the community of disciples in this age. Correspondingly, the promise of being first was an equally accurate and appropriate epitome of the blessedness of heirs of God's Kingdom.

This being true, the implicit theology of this aphorism reinforces what we have said earlier of other commands. For instance, the aphorism is credible only if it truly expresses the will of God. Otherwise no one takes it seriously. And no saying more deftly illustrates the conviction that God's thoughts are different from man's thoughts (cf. Isa. 55:8). Many religions, to be sure, utilize their gods to support social and institutional interests, further rewarding those who have become first; but in doing so they exemplify the essence of idolatry. According to this axiom, the true God wills to undermine this idolatry at its very source in self-interest.

The proverb implies also that making the last first is God's *work* as well as his *will.* "God opposes the proud, but gives grace to the humble." (James 4:6; Prov. 3:34; I Peter 5:5; I Clem. 30:2; Ign. Eph. 5:3; Clem. Alex. Strom. III. 6.) This is an Old Testament saying which was later falsely attributed to Jesus.[4] Moreover, this work of God is central, not peripheral, to his saving purpose in dealing with his people, always reflecting the truth "My ways are not your ways" (cf. Isa. 55:8). No religious establishment can ever amend this article in the constitution of the Kingdom nor control the direction of God's action in history.

This aphorism, with its intrinsic antithesis, implies the continuing conflict between God and idols, or between God and Satan. The realm of Satan is as clearly defined by implication as the realm of God, for the saying in its most succinct form (Matt. 20:16) describes the boundary between the two realms. One realm is the place where the first are recognized as first and receive their reward; the opposing realm is constituted by the recognitions given to the last. The gate into this realm has over it the warning: "Unless you . . . , you will never enter the kingdom of heaven" (Matt. 18:3). To this latter realm, therefore, the warning imparts a due sense of mystery, for here there takes place a transfiguration of all prior conceptions of power, prestige, privilege, and protocol. What later scholars have called eschatology refers at least in part to efforts to clarify the junction and disjunction of those two realms. The imperative of Jesus functioned in such a way as to station his disciples on that boundary, where damnation and salvation depended on their most secret desires. Did his demand require an impossible action? That could be tested only by their response. They could not understand the range of the possible until they had tried to enter this narrowest of all gates.

The character of this choice colored every practice of the early church, especially its liturgical life. We have seen how the choice confronted every Christian as he prayed, fasted, or gave alms (Matt. 6:1-6, 16-18). In this chapter we have

[4] Cf. W. D. Stroker, "The Formation of Secondary Sayings of Jesus," Ph.D. Dissertation, Yale University, 1970, pp. 40-41.

seen how the proverb gravitated toward sacramental contexts. To be baptized signaled the readiness to become last (Mark 10:35-45) and simultaneously the willingness to wash one another's feet and to drink the cup. Both private and communal worship were ways of becoming last. The early church could in fact be defined as the community which God called into being by issuing this demand and fulfilling this promise. Moreover, the history of the proverb illustrates the role of Jesus in the creation of this community. That role was many-sided: teacher, revealer, forgiver, mediator, judge, exemplar, atoning sacrifice, victor over Satan and death. The proverb in its various incarnations within the life of the early church embodies all those roles. It stands as an excellent epitome not so much of christological doctrine as of christological action among men, both before and after the death of Jesus.

6 Sell and Give

The cross he bore is life and health
Tho' shame and death to him,
His people's hope, his people's wealth,
Their everlasting theme.

Thomas Kelly

In the previous essay we studied the requirement to surrender all kinds of social status, a step which leaves the individual followers no rights but only duties vis-à-vis others. One way of fulfilling this requirement was a voluntary acceptance of poverty. In a key passage in Mark and Matthew (Mark 10:17-31; Matt. 19:16-30) lastness was seen to be the status of a man who had abandoned house, brothers, sisters, parents, children, and fields on account of the gospel. This understanding of the situation was expressed in the conflation of Mark 10:31 with the preceding unit. Those who are last have given up every possession in order to follow Jesus. The rich man of Mark 10:17-22 refused to make that sacrifice. Disciples and rich man thus function as negative and positive exemplars of the principle enunciated in the famous hyperbole

It is easier for a camel to go through the eye of a needle than for a rich man to enter the kingdom of God.[1] (*Matt. 10:25.*)

[1] For a fuller analysis of the history of this teaching, cf. my essay "The Needle's Eye," *JBL* 61 (1942): 157-69; also E. Best, "The Camel and the Needle's Eye," *Expository Times* 82 (1970): 83-88.

Few sayings of Jesus are more radical than his hyperbole of the camel going through the needle's eye. But to the historian the primary problem is not that of the definition and application of Jesus' saying for our own day. Rather it is the reconstruction of the various stages in the developing tradition and the clarification of the function of the unit in each of these stages. For wherever an accretion can be isolated, it provides a clue to a concrete situation in early Christian experience.

When one applies the test of form to this block of material, he immediately notices signs of elaborate development, for pure examples of the major forms of oral tradition are absent. It is neither a proverb nor paraenesis, neither paradigm nor legend, although traces of each of these exist. It is far more circumstantial, elaborate, more of a connected dialogue, than most units of didactic purpose. The very corruptness of the form suggests the presence of accretions. Particularly suspect is the interest in secondary characters, in their status, their personal relation to Jesus, their emotions, their fates. Raise but once the question, "Did this entire section (Mark 10:17-31) circulate during several decades of oral transmission precisely in this form and without alteration?" and doubts are inescapable. But if there has been alteration, must there not be some trace of its nature and extent? Can the earliest nuclei be recovered and the process of growth reconstructed? Accretions after the date of Mark can be demonstrated; must they not have occurred before Mark? Surely so, yet to chart the history of this diffuse and multi-motivated tradition is not easy. For the period before Mark, the criteria of judgment are inherently subjective and incapable of proof; consequently no more than a probable hypothesis can be hoped for.

Even so, there are clear signs of a structural pattern in the three paragraphs of Mark 10:17-31: (1) a basic rule, stated with prophetic rigor in the image of camel/needle (the kernel of vss. 23-27); (2) the example of a man who failed the test (vss. 17-22); (3) the example of men who passed it (vss. 28-31). Before examining those paragraphs more closely, however, let us look at the basic motifs which pervade the longer segment of Mark to which these three paragraphs belong.

A thread of continuity suggests itself in the long chain of materials reaching from 10:13 to 11:10. One antithesis pervades the whole. It is the recurring contrast between the humble and the exalted, the poor and the rich, the last and the first, the least and the greatest, those who serve and those who are served. Excluding our passage from consideration, we find many illustrations of this antithesis:

one must become as lowly as a child in order to enter the Kingdom (10:13-16);
the Son of man must humble himself on the road to exaltation (10:32-34);
his disciples must drink the same cup (10:38-39);
Gentile standards of power are opposite the standards of the Kingdom (10:42-43);
Jesus' death establishes the pattern of service (10:43-45);
the blind man recognizes the meaning of Jesus' passion (10:46-52), but his disciples do not;
the entry into Jerusalem dramatizes the meekness of the Messiah (11:1-10).

In terms of the mission of Jesus, the entire chain illustrates the truth of Paul's affirmation: "Though he was rich, yet for your sake he became poor" (II Cor. 8:9). The teaching on wealth and the contrast between disciples and non-disciples in our passage (10:17-31) fits this Markan perspective. They illustrate the antithesis between meekness and pride which the mission of Jesus had burned into the memories of his followers. The appearance of the floating proverb as the conclusion of our block of material is evidence of this homogeneity, for this very proverb could apply to every link in the chain of pericopes from 10:13 to 11:10. "Many that are first will be last, and the last first" (10:31).

The Rich Man

Turning now to the story of the rich man, let us look for that nucleus around which the rest of the story may have developed. Here the introductory link in vs. 17*a* and the transition link in vs. 23*a* seem to be editorial tissue and nothing more. The first of these locates the whole discussion on the road leading to Jerusalem, that road which symbolized the solidarity of true disciples with the passion of Jesus. The rich man wished to worship this teacher (he "knelt before him"), but he was not ready to follow on the path which entailed the surrender of all possessions. The transition in 23*a* shows clearly that, in an unknown editor's mind, the story of the rich man's failure functioned to demonstrate to the Twelve not only what this same "way" required of them, but also what they must say to similar inquirers after Jesus' death. These editorial touches are consistent with the earlier tradition without being an integral part of it.

In the episode of the rich man there are three possible nuclei of tradition. Verse 18 stresses the sole goodness of God. This teaching is in itself important and has many corollaries in early Christian faith. It reflects the Pauline attitude toward man's sinfulness and toward Jesus' humble status; it implies a rejection of the Pharisaic conception of merits and underscores complete dependence upon the grace of God. But this idea is clearly not the central core of the story as a whole, around which the other materials gravitated, even though it does suggest how fully Jesus himself embodied the "poverty" of spirit which could pass through the eye of the needle.

A second possible nucleus is the *double* answer to the rich man's query on how to inherit eternal life. "First obey the law, then give to the poor," legal righteousness plus self-chosen poverty. This answer is reminiscent of the Matthean "Unless your righteousness exceeds that of the scribes and Pharisees, you will never enter the kingdom of heaven" (cf. esp. Matt. 5:17-20; 23:2-3). But two considerations prevent the acceptance of this double answer as the original core. One is the consideration of content; the other that of form. The content of this teaching contradicts the emphasis of other teachings which are indisputably original. For inherent in this double answer is the acceptance of legal standards of justification: the man is a good man and is therefore the object of Jesus' love. Only one thing he lacks—the sacrifice of his wealth. Would this be a gospel of good news to publicans and sinners, to require them to obey the commandments and then to sacrifice all their wealth? Is this demand congruous with the assurance of the Kingdom as God's gift to his little flock, to the meek and the suffering? Does this ring true to his message of forgiveness, to his mission to those aware of their inability to keep the Torah? The emphasis upon keeping the Mosaic law is not characteristic of units two and three, nor of the larger context in Mark. Nor is it necessarily implied in the concluding and decisive demand, "Go . . . sell . . . give . . . follow."

The suspicion suggested by considerations of content is supported by considerations of form. To the same question two answers are given, and between the two there is no necessary connection. Either could serve as the nucleus of a paradigm. In fact, each answer did circulate by itself, for close parallels to each have been preserved in gospel tradition. In the relatively pure paradigm of Luke 10:25-28, a lawyer raises the same question: "Teacher, what shall I do to inherit eternal life?" And Jesus' answer is, "What is written in the Law? . . . Do this, and you will live." The quotation from the Law is different, but structurally the answers are similar. And in the possible doublet of Mark 12:28-34, a scribe asks concerning the first commandment and agrees with Jesus' answer. Moreover, Jesus' answer, "You are not far from the kingdom of God," is curiously similar to his answer in our story, "you lack one thing" (Mark 10:21). We have already noted the parallels in thought to Matthew's emphasis upon righteousness over and above the Law.

As for analogies to the second answer, "Go . . . sell . . . give . . . follow," the tradition supplies many.

Sell your possessions, and give alms; provide yourselves with purses that do not grow old, with a treasure in the heavens that does not fail. (*Luke 12:33.*)

Give to every one who begs from you; and of him who takes away your goods, do not ask them again. (*Luke 6:30.*)

Consider also the Lukan beatitudes and woes, and the parables of Dives/Lazarus, the rich fool, the unrighteous steward, and the stringent call for disciples to deny themselves (Luke 14:25-27; 17:33; Mark 8:34-35). This element is, as we shall see, the only link to the teaching of the succeeding units (Mark 10:23-31).

This second command of Jesus, "Go . . . sell . . . give . . . follow," then, is much the most intelligible selection as the primitive core for the story of the rich man. Assuming that it is the earliest core, let us recapitulate the major stages in the growth of the story. In embryo, it begins as a radical demand for voluntary poverty, for complete severance from the ties of this age, for seeking only the rewards which God gives in the coming age. In content it is germane to the eschatological situation, with its reversal of normal standards of security and power. In form it is a condensed axiomatic demand circulating orally among the disciples of Jesus in the earliest Jerusalem community, perfectly congenial to their outlook and practice.

This demand then attracts to itself a minimum narrative context to increase its intelligibility. A non-disciple asks the question, "What must I do to inherit eternal life?" and the axiomatic demand provides the answer, "Go . . . sell . . . give . . . follow." Verse 17 and verse 21*b* combined to form a tiny paradigm, complete and intelligible, similar to other miniature paradigms that dot the Gospel pages. This addition facilitates the use of the teaching in instructing converts and in preaching to penitent seekers of the Kingdom. There is only one clause which breaks the sequence in this tiny paradigm: "You will have treasure in heaven." This clause is precisely the same as in many other primitive commands where the renunciation of earthly status assured the grant of heavenly compensation.

In Jewish-Christian communities this same question (What shall I do?) was a popular one that had received various answers, some of which dealt specifically with the requirement that disciples fulfill the Law. These answers would be most germane in a time when the addition of gentile converts had provoked the legal controversy. They would circulate in communities that were still predominantly Jewish. What was more natural than that these two answers to the same question, both present in the same community, should gravitate together and be conflated? To inherit the Kingdom one must both fulfill the Law and sacrifice everything in becoming a disciple (vss. 17*b*-21). The heavier accent remains on the necessity of voluntary poverty as the special distinction of discipleship. That accent indicates that this step took place in the milieu of primitive Jewish-Christian communities.

The next steps consist of the elaboration of details concerning the questioner, details which enhance the accent just noted. The petitioner is pictured as a good man, by Pharisaic standards, and a rich one. He is eager, respectful, righteous, and even lovable, *but*. . . . The fact that he fufills one requirement underscores his failure to fulfill the other. Like Zacchaeus and like the wealthy publicans and sinners, he might have accepted the requirement, and yet his refusal makes the central demand of vs. 21 all the more decisive and suggests why publicans and sinners precede the Pharisees and scribes into the Kingdom. Even with these circumstantial additions the milieu remains that of a Jewish community within which the band of disciples had been made conscious of its separateness.

Verse 18 is the only element in the story which seems unrelated to the primitive nucleus of vs. 21*b*. One possible relationship to the unit seems to be verbal, i.e., the word "good." In the mind of some hearers the address "Good teacher" called from memory a proverb concerning the goodness of God. Another possibility is more subtle still. The implicit contrast between this man who was both rich and good, and

Jesus who was neither, may have added to the force of the command. This teacher was poor enough and humble enough to speak with authority.

After the story received a literary anchorage in Mark, it continued to grow, though probably at a slower pace. The changes in Matthew 19 and in the Gospel of the Hebrews are worthy of attention. Four changes in Matthew may be noted. The editor revises the question from "Good teacher" to "What good deed" in order to remove a supposed blemish from the character of the Master. Borrowing from other traditions of Jesus' sayings, he adds to the Decalogue requirements the command "You shall love your neighbor as yourself" to make the standard of legal righteousness more comprehensive. More important still, he reveals his contentment with the legal standard by making it completely adequate: "If you would enter life, keep the commandments." As a result, the call for voluntary poverty may be addressed primarily to those whom Jesus wanted to send into the mission field (Matt. 10:5 ff.) and who therefore needed to surrender families and homes for the sake of proclaiming the gospel (Mark 10:29; Matt. 19:28-29). Incidentally, the editor makes the older man of Mark 10:20 a young man, a change that was possibly due to an accidental misunderstanding of the Markan phrase "from my youth."

These alterations are consonant with well-known legalistic tendencies in Matthew. They point to the need in a well-developed Jewish-Christian church for regular catechetical instruction of Christians and for a new law that would fulfill Pharisaic standards and still preserve the distinctive status of Christians as separate from the synagogue. The radicalism of the original teaching, oriented toward an in-breaking Kingdom, gives way to the practical need for a reliable norm in a church accommodating itself to survival in this age.

Though the Gospel of the Nazaraeans reveals acquaintance with the Matthean form of the story, the basic answer is quite different. As in Matthew, the form of the question is similar: "What good thing must I do that I may live?" A legendary accretion is present in the picture of the rich man scratching his head. More important, however, is the refusal to separate in Matthean fashion the norm for salvation and the norm for perfection. Charity becomes the real test of legal righteousness. When the rich man affirms that he has kept the law, Jesus flatly contradicts him.

How canst thou say, I have fulfilled the law and the prophets? For it stands written in the law: Love thy neighbour as thyself; and behold, many of thy brethren, sons of Abraham, are begrimed with dirt and die of hunger—and thy house is full of many good things and nothing at all comes forth from it to them! [2]

Is this picture of the rich man affected by the story of Dives? Perhaps. At least, the milieu remains that of Jewish Christianity where the problem of church-synagogue relationships is uppermost, and where charity has become a regular duty of Christians.

The Camel

In the next paragraph (Mark 10:23-27), there is only one real kernel, vs. 25. Once this kernel is identified, the subsequent expansion of the teaching is almost obvious.

> It is easier for a camel to go through the eye of a needle
> than for a rich man to enter the kingdom of God.

Practically all commentators accept the primitiveness of this saying, although they frequently modify its stringency. Several factors support its classification as primitive. It illustrates the rule that the most difficult reading, whether the difficulty be stylistic or ethical, is likely to be the earliest. It is so difficult a saying that it has created a problem for the church from that day to this. It must have had pristine authority to have been preserved; it is hard to imagine any early Christian creating it. In fact, every change in the tradition tends to weaken the effect of the saying. In content, this statement is

[2] P. Vielhauer in Hennecke—Schneemelcher—Wilson, *New Testament Apocrypha,* I (Philadelphia: The Westminster Press, 1963) : 149.

entirely consistent with other sayings of Jesus concerning wealth, and with the commands on other matters which view earthly social rewards and heavenly divine rewards as mutually exclusive. The imagery is drawn from Jewish tradition and would be entirely clear to the rural folk of Galilee. In form, the saying is a hyperbole such as Jesus frequently used.[3] How much more characteristic of the prophetic utterances of Jesus than the prosaic "how hard it will be" of vs. 23!

In comparison, vss. 23 and 24 are strangely weak and have often been suspected by commentators as secondary. They are unimaginative explanations of the obvious meaning of the hyperbole. Verse 23 may be an editorial redundancy to provide a link to the preceding unit, or it may be intended as a conclusion to the story of the rich man. In either case it is suspect. In vs. 24 according to some manuscripts the hyperbole is further weakened by the phrase "who trust in riches," which makes the needle's eye very much larger. This phrase may be a textual gloss or it may be an accretion during pre-Markan development; in either case its motive is clear and its secondary character obvious. Verse 24 should perhaps be placed after vs. 25, as in Ms. D, but that makes no difference in the interpretation of its origin and function. The lateness of both 23 and 24 is further indicated by the question in 26. These later verses assume the sheer human impossibility, not the great difficulty, of rich men entering the Kingdom. Had vss. 23 and 24 been a part of the unit from the beginning, there would have been little need to include the question "Then who can be saved?"

Having noted the secondary character of vss. 23 and 24, let us look more closely at the discussion of impossibility. "Then who can be saved?" This is a question which the hyperbole of Jesus has always provoked in a group in which rich men are prominent. But is it a question that would naturally arise among the disciples of Jesus or in the earliest Jerusalem community? Would the twelve, who had sacrificed everything

[3] In this case he chose the largest animal normally seen in Palestine and the smallest conceivable opening. (Cf. E. Best, "The Camel and the Needle's Eye," p. 88.)

in order to follow Jesus, have raised this query? Or imagine the distressed poor of Galilee to whom Jesus proclaimed the gospel worrying about the exclusion of the rich or wondering if anyone could be saved! And if the picture of the Jerusalem church is accurately given in Acts and in Paul's letters, it is likewise incredible that they should have been greatly disturbed by this hyperbole, for they were already poverty-stricken. The very formation of the question indicates that an earlier teaching, one that had become authoritative in itself because of its supposed author, has been transmitted to a new setting in which it creates a problem, for now there are Christians whom the saying of Jesus confronts with a step which seems to be impossible.

If the question of Mark 10:26 is secondary, so is the answer given in vs. 27. To be sure, when it is freed from this context, the assurance that all things are possible with God remains intact. The origin of this assurance may lie in an entirely different context. The idea is frequently found in the Old Testament and may have been culled thence by Christians to meet the problem of how rich men can enter the Kingdom. More probably the saying was drawn directly from Christian tradition itself. Disciples recognized that the Kingdom's approach represented a human impossibility; it could come only as a miraculous gift. Men must have faith in the impossible and pray, never doubting. With faith, mountains could be cast into the sea. If we cut the artificial link between this assurance in vs. 27 and the hyperbole of the needle's eye, we find many possibilities of interpretation akin to other teachings of Jesus. But vs. 27 does not belong to this setting. As Prof. Best observes, "Mark was but the first to have turned the edge of a hard saying by transforming it into a theological proposition." [4]

We can thus conjecture the history of this hyperbole in oral tradition. It begins as an authentic echo of Jesus' eschatological radicalism (vs. 25). Then its difficulty is recognized by a well-to-do community of Christians who raise the ques-

[4] *Ibid.*, p. 84.

tion "Then who can be saved?" They find the answer in a comforting assurance of what is possible to God (vss. 26, 27). A prosaic and redundant introduction is then added which further emasculates the hyperbole (vs. 23). Then the teaching is further qualified by being applied to those "who trust in riches." This sequence of changes becomes an instructive example of the process of Christian casuistry, modifying the tradition during successive generations.

The Disciples

In the third paragraph (vss. 28-31) the kernel saying is more difficult to identify because changes have permeated every section of the teaching. Most clearly peripheral is the concluding proverb (vs. 31) in that it appears in so many different contexts that it is difficult to assign its origin to any one. Here it is easily excised, though its genuineness need not thereby be disputed. Verse 28 is an editorial connective in Markan idiom which is not integral to the saying. The teaching is not limited to Peter, since he speaks for the Twelve and the answer is directed to them. The saying itself, however, embraces an even larger audience: "no one."

So we are left with the teaching of vss. 29 and 30. In these two nuclear verses one may detect evidences of post-resurrection situations. There is the explicit reference to persecutions, the technical Christian language of the phrase "for my sake and the gospel's sake," the implicit reference to the church as providing a new family for those who have broken away from home, the sharp distinction between rewards during this age and those of the coming age, and the detailed description of sacrifices that would apply to almost any Christian during the apostolic age. For one who places a premium on discovering secondary accretions, this paragraph offers ample opportunity for the display of his ingenuity. Any effort to trace a particular phrase to the precise words of Jesus is certain to be greeted by skepticism. Yet there is good reason for being skeptical of such skepticism.

To sum up, then, both in form and in content, the camel

proverb with its stark absoluteness parallels many other sayings which must be considered authentic. The command in vs. 21 certainly harmonizes with other expressions of the earliest calls for disciples, whether or not the tradition has preserved detailed examples of such calls. There is no reason to doubt that as a result of Jesus' explosive message some men did break loose from ties to house and family and fields. There is, in fact, every reason to believe that he promised them rewards from God for each voluntary surrender of social securities and status. Intrinsic to many of his teachings is the prophetic disclosure of the smallness of the needle's eye and the abundance of the Kingdom's riches, e.g., the "hundredfold" of vs. 30. In short, the structural pattern which gives coherence to this tradition, whether in its earlier or its later stages, rings true to patterns we have detected elsewhere. The theme of the beatitudes and woes is here stated in the form of hyperbole and of command and promise, with illustrations of each. Discipleship requires total sacrifice. To enter the future age one must join the lost, the least, the last, the poor, the meek, those who have surrendered their entire stake in the present age. This principle is too deeply grounded in the tradition, too pervasive in all strands to be other than very early. It preserves a dominant accent in Jesus' proclamation of the Kingdom's approach: threat for the wealthy, proud, privileged, self-sufficient, righteous ones; promise for the poor, humble, dispossessed, ostracized, sinful.

The absoluteness and rigor of this message cannot and should not be obscured. Enduring significance does not depend upon turning Jesus' separate sayings into a final norm practicable for all men at all times. Significance lies rather in the fact that his message cannot be forced into the rigid categories of laws adapted to an institution designed to regularize social forces in the present age. Why must we continue to analyze the personality of the rich man, psychologize the motives of Jesus, and rationalize the dangers of wealth? Only because we assume that in the hyperbole we have an authoritative canon which, to be accepted, must be domesticated within the customary behavior of a religious community. If instead we grasp these teachings as signs of the Kingdom's nearness, as reflections of its revolutionary character, as implications of what happens when that transcendence breaks in upon the relativities of empirical history, then they become luminous with new and deeper meanings.

Perspective

Last, we should say something about the theological perspective which inheres in this teaching. There is little to add here to what was said in the previous chapters. The imperatives "go, sell, give" are so similar to the commands to love, to lend, to give alms, to renounce rewards from men, that they reflect the same basic conception of God's will and ways, the same understanding of how God's Kingdom impinges on man's decisions, the same black-and-white contrast between opposing sovereignties, and the same revolutionary rejection of those securities which constitute the infra-structure of economic and religious systems. These are common to the manifold strands of the teaching tradition in their earliest stages.

This particular strand, however, does disclose a very distinctive accent. The command given to the rich man in all three Synoptics reaches a certain climax in the words "Follow me." Moreover the Synoptics agree that the dialogue prompted by this command proceeds between Jesus and those who have determined to follow him. The fact that Matthew brought into this context the promise of twelve thrones (19:28) shows that he understood that this dialogue was most appropriate to the small group of men chosen to rule the twelve tribes of Israel. If his understanding of Mark is correct, and I think it is, then we may draw certain inferences concerning the primitive conceptions of the church.

For example, Jesus called for followers with the intention of creating a community of those who valued the Kingdom above all else. To seek eternal life (Mark 10:17, 30) and to follow Jesus were linked together from the very beginning. We are dealing, then, not with generalized moral teaching but with a specific "campaign." The choice lies between two distinct communities, two sets of brothers and sisters. Moreover, within that new community which was granted by God in exchange for the houses forsaken, a necessary role is accorded to rulers and teachers. Their role required at least two things: their own passage through the needle's eye and their readiness to require the same passage on the part of all would-be followers. The addition of the first/last axiom in Mark 10:31 is extraordinarily fitting in that it shows not only the basis of belonging within the new community (becoming last) but also the basis of hierarchical ministry within that community (becoming first). This tradition therefore encourages us to conclude that even before his Passion Jesus brought into existence both a community of adherents and a smaller band of leaders for that community. Perhaps the historian should doubt the degree of continuity between this and the community which in later centuries was still called the church, but he should not doubt the emergence of such a community during the ministry of Jesus. Otherwise he would be unable to explain either the origin or the preservation of such prophetic declarations as this one about the camel.

7 Ask, Seek, Knock

Hope is the pillar of the world.
Zulu Proverb

No teaching of Jesus created more frequent echoes or more profound reverberations in early Christian circles than this triple command and promise. Often overlooked, often relegated to innocuous homilies on prayer, these verses will repay thorough examination.

Form A—1. Ask, and it will be given you
2. Seek, and you will find
3. Knock, and it will be opened to you
(*Matt. 7:7; Luke 11:9.*)

The form of this triplet is so transparent as to require little comment. The jewel is so symmetrical as to prompt a sense of wonder at the artistry of construction. Each command is a single-word imperative that addresses readers directly and in the plural. Each imperative is followed by a promise issued to that audience, a promise that utilizes a verb which complements the action, e.g., a person knocks at a door, the appropriate response is the opening of the door to welcome the "outsider." The economy in the use of words is amazing. There are only twenty words in English, and these translate no more than eleven words in Greek. Each of the three lines can stand alone in complete independence. Yet in the combination, each reinforces and interprets the others, like the three sides of an equilateral triangle. The combination leads the audience (and here we must remember that these teachings were used orally, moving directly from the lips of a speaker to the ears of a company gathered about him) to treat the three commands as a single command to be followed by a single action, an action described by knocking as aptly as by seeking or asking. In a similar way the triple promise becomes a triple way of expressing a single reward for that single action.

So symmetrical is the triangle that it is easy in oral communication to shift the accent from one angle to another. The command can be stressed, as if the most urgent matter were to move an unwilling audience from passivity to action. The promise can be stressed, as if to imply that an audience which has acted in the way commanded can have full confidence in ample returns, quite contrary to manifest probabilities. So, too, the accent can shift from one of the commands to another, depending upon how a current audience visualizes itself—as engaged in a hunt, on a pilgrimage, or in prayer. A hundred or a thousand specific situations are covered by these self-images. The teaching can apply with minimum alteration as a popular axiom to the general public, or as a mark of special privilege to a religious cell, or as a guide to action on the part of the individual believer (although this would involve treating the plural *you* as a distributive plural, which most modern readers unwisely do).

The triple command is at once highly specific and universal in its range of concern, and yet a baffling feature is its ambiguity at decisive points. Who is issuing this command, to whom, and on whose authority What resources has he for implementing his assurances? Does the promise apply equally to all forms of asking and all kinds of knocking? Are no conditions attached to the fulfillment of the promise, other than obedience to the command? Does it focus upon individual or corporate action? And by what specific actions would a community embody its obedience? Is the teaching equally applicable to all situations, audiences, and requests? If not, under what circumstances does the command become obligatory? Should one assume that what will be given corresponds precisely to what is asked? When one reviews all these questions which are provoked by Form A, he may well treat the teaching as a riddle, shaped for the very purpose of creating bewilderment. The meaning which at first seems to be visible on the surface keeps receding to depths beyond the reach of critical analysis, with no clear clues to what should be asked or received. The context becomes absolutely decisive for limiting the meaning, yet the saying itself gives no indication as to the most appropriate context.

Form B—1. For every one who asks receives
2. And he who seeks finds
3. And to him who knocks it will be opened
(*Matt. 7:8; Luke 11:10.*)

Here occurs an abrupt shift in form; the command-promise becomes an indicative assertion of a general rule. This rule is shaped to correspond to Form A. Word by word, line by line, the parallel structure is polished to maximum brevity and smoothness. Only two slight alterations occur. Plurals are replaced by singulars: "every one." And the verb of the promise in A 1 ("it will be given") becomes in B 1 "receives." This shift from passive to active may diminish the importance of the giver. Judgments will differ concerning the effects of shifting from the imperative-promissory type of statement in Form A to the assertive-indicative type of statement in Form B. Does it relax the pressure for decision on the part of the seeker and thus strengthen the likelihood that he will postpone action until he has debated whether or not to accept the principle? Does Form A provoke personal confrontation where, by contrast, Form B invites impersonal speculation? Does Form A encourage action as immediate personal response to personal address, whereas Form B encourages intellectual endorsement of an abstract principle? To hazard answers to such questions is an elusive business. But it should be obvious that the reference of B is as ambiguous as A. B does not help us define more precisely the content of A, but sounds like an innocuous and unnecessary restatement. For practical purposes, therefore, we can ignore B in our subsequent analysis. Let us make one final observation. It is remarkable that the

Matthean and Lukan versions of Forms A and B are identical. A total of twenty-four Greek words appears in the same order and with precisely the same forms—a remarkable phenomenon. From this point on, however, the two Gospels vary so widely that we must use parallel columns to show both versions.

Form C

1. Or what man of you	1. What father among you
2. if his son asks him for a loaf	2. if his son asks for a fish (4)
3. will give him a stone?	3. will . . . give him a serpent? (5)
4. Or if he asks for a fish (2)	4. Or if he asks for an egg
5. will give him a serpent? (3)	5. will give him a scorpion?
6. If you then who are evil	6. If you then who are evil
7. know how to give good gifts to your children	7. know how to give good gifts to your children
8. how much more will your Father who is in heaven	8. how much more will the heavenly Father
9. give good things to those who ask him?	9. give the Holy Spirit to those who ask him?
(*Matt. 7:9-11.*)	(*Luke 11:11-13.*)

The structure of these questions in the two Gospels is the same. There are, however some interesting variants. In lines 2-5 different requests are made: bread and fish in Matthew, fish and egg in Luke. Different objects are indicated as bad or useless gifts: stone and serpent in Matthew, serpent and scorpion in Luke. In line 8 there is a slight difference in the way of referring to the heavenly Father. A more substantial change occurs in line 9 where the Father gives the Holy Spirit in Luke and good things in Matthew, the latter preserving a closer parallel to line 7.

These variants help to define potential contexts for Form A. For instance, bread and fish were from earliest times staple items in the common meals of the house churches, and especially in the eucharistic celebrations. From early stages in the gospel tradition these two items served as profound symbols of the Messianic presence (cf. the feeding of the 5,000 and the 4,000). These Matthean touches suggest more clearly a connection between Form A and the liturgical situation, including the petitions offered there. That the asking and receiving should involve the Holy Spirit reflects Luke's concern for that gift which he considered essential to the life of the church, as contrasted to the serpent and scorpion, symbols of the demonic enemies from which man needs to be saved.

We should notice how the addition of these rhetorical questions served to narrow the circle of meaning of Form A. It is altogether likely that Form C had become fused with Form AB before the composition of Matthew and Luke. That fact, however, does not preclude the possibility that at an earlier stage Form C had not yet been joined to Form A and B. While Form C provides an apt illustration of asking (A-1 and B 1), it throws less light on the action of seeking and knocking (A 2, 3, B 2, 3). We need therefore to imagine A and B first circulating separately in oral tradition, and we must ask how the addition of Form C modified the force of Form A. The major modification is the removal of several of the ambiguities. The identities of the asker and the giver become clearer. The *you* of Form A is now seen to mean sons of the heavenly Father, members of his family, bound to him in a relationship which is even closer and stronger than natural family ties. The giver and opener are now identified as the heavenly Father, known by the sons, remembered by them as one to whom they had entrusted all their hopes for the future. Whatever had happened earlier between this Father and this community of sons can now be assumed to provide background and basis for the command.

The fact that the parable (Form C) focuses on the command to ask is significant. It chooses the act of prayer as the proper context for interpreting all three commands. Luke says this more clearly than Matthew does, because he places this whole pericope in sequence with two other teachings on prayer (11:1-8). More than this, Form C implies that these sons have little difficulty in obeying the commands of Form A. They have greater difficulty in trusting the triple promise of Form A and the rule of Form B. The parable is told to elicit such confidence. As a result, the force of the exhortation is weakened, while that of the performative statement is strengthened. This points to a community which finds it hard to believe in the promise. Why? Probably because it was finding it difficult to survive. At least this reason is suggested in the choice of bread and fish, the everyday, cheap minimal diet for survival in Palestine. Moreover, we may conjecture that these particular sons of the Father were having survival problems because of their loyalty to his will. Social and economic stress had given them abundant reason to doubt the dependability of Form B. Presumably such doubts would show up in their prayers. Bound to ask for bread and fish, they had the same loss of courage as the Twelve in the wilderness when they were asked to feed 5,000 with bread and fish. In other words, the addition of Form C here shifts the interpretation of Form A in the direction of Matt. 6:8, 11, 26*c*, 30, and Luke 11:3, 5-8. The addition of Form C also makes the thrust of Form A more individual than corporate. Since this addition probably took place in the stage of oral transmission, we conclude that already during that early stage teachers felt the need to make the force of Form A less ambiguous by applying it to situations being experienced by the churches. We can thus detect in Form C one of the many examples of primitive exegesis of Form A. But there are other examples, and to locate them we will look first for several interpretations of "knocking" and "seeking" in order to compensate for the overemphasis on "asking" which Form C produced.

A 3—Knock, and It Will Be Opened to You

When we search for occurrences of this image which may throw light on the meaning of Form A as a whole, there is an embarrassment of riches. A whole constellation of pictures is involved; for the act of knocking involves doors and gates, keys, the role of porter or watchman, the house or the fold, entrance or exclusion. Knocking was but one way of connoting the search for salvation. Door and keys were popular images of success in that search (Matt. 23:13). Men experienced a continuing struggle between the gates of heaven and the gates of hell (Matt. 16:18), and at every point along the path to the Kingdom a pilgrim had to choose between those two gates (Matt. 7:13-14). Disciples faced the real danger of exclusion from the gates of heaven, for the road was strenuous (Matt. 7:14) and the master would exclude some who were entirely confident of admission (Matt. 7:23; 25:10-12). Viewing his life through these pictures, no disciple could interpret the promise of A 3 as operating in any mechanical or automatic way. He knew that knocking was no casual, momentary, or halfhearted action. In his world the opening of the door represented a miraculous transformation from imprisonment to freedom, from frustration to fulfillment (Acts 5:19; 14:27; I Cor. 16:9; II Cor. 2:12; Rev. 3:8). The gate or the door symbolized both the nearness and the distance from salvation, for the kingdom of God was "at the doors" (Matt. 24:33; 25:10; Jas. 5:9). Just as knocking represented his deepest and most urgent desire, so, too, the opening of the door represented entrance into life and full participation in the joys of the Lord. The act of knocking may be understood as roughly analogous to the longing expressed in the first line of the Advent hymn: "O come, O come, Emmanuel, and ransom captive Israel." Similarly, the promise conveyed an assurance analogous to the last line of the hymn: "Emmanuel shall come to thee, O Israel." With that possibility in mind, let us look with greater detail at four passages which indicate various early interpretations of knocking and opening.

(1) The parable in Luke 13:23-30 is quite typical. It seems to be addressed to a general audience of Jewish folk in various towns and villages as Jesus and his disciples were journeying toward Jerusalem; this setting signified to Luke the impending consummation in that city of Jesus' ministry (9:51-52). This setting gave urgency to the saying, for the time was very near when the door would be shut and the opportunity to enter would be lost. The Jerusalem route also underscored the contrast between the many seekers who would not be admitted and the few who would. The narrowness of the door was defined by the rigors of a discipleship which entailed accompanying the Messiah to his death (13:31-35). The

doorkeeper, who had full power to open the closed door, represented the Lord himself. Inside the door the tables were spread in the kingdom of God, with a guest list consisting of patriarchs and prophets, along with men who had been drawn from all points of the compass. Readers are left in little doubt about what the door's opening connotes. The accent falls upon the threat of exclusion, not on the promise of inclusion. This threat is leveled at men who had eaten with Jesus; they therefore expected to be welcomed, not rebuffed, by him. Their striving to enter is commanded as a way of avoiding this rebuff. In this context striving takes the form of readiness to make a total sacrifice as required by this Master (e.g., 14:25-33). The key image is the act of knocking, as in A 3, but the use made of it is strikingly different. In this case the emphasis falls not on the promise but on the command to knock. How many will be willing to knock in time, inasmuch as knocking means dying with Christ?

(2) Another context as offered by another parable produces a variant interpretation of the basic principle (Luke 11:5-8). As the immediate sequel to the Lord's Prayer, its placement here is possibly an illustration of the petition "Give us each day our daily bread." As the teaching appearing immediately prior to Form A, this parable illustrates both the asking and the knocking of A 1, 3. The actors in this vignette are three friends. The request in this case is for bread, not, to be sure, for their own use but for a hungry guest. The reason for opening the door and giving the bread is not friendship but need. Both the knocker and the opener are motivated by the need of the traveler. At least for Luke, the generosity of the opener is seen to be analogous to God's grace. In fact, Form A can be viewed very easily as the moral that concludes this parable which, like what follows in Form C, stresses the dependability of the triple promise rather than the difficulty of the triple command. It is easy for a hungry man to ask for bread, but remarkable that he receives it. The emphasis may be due to the reference here to prayer rather than, as in 13:23-30, to the readiness to sacrifice everything as the price of discipleship.

(3) The symbolic possibilities of the door are much more highly developed in John 10:1-18. This multi-layered discourse discloses how many allusions the image released in the imaginative world of early Christians. Here the act of entrance connotes not only the once-for-all salvation but also the daily passage to and from the pasturelands. The gate symbolizes both the shepherd and the path by which the shepherd leads the flock. It is the character of this gate which distinguishes the true shepherd from competing thieves and robbers. There is a gatekeeper, whose voice is decisive for the sheep because his knowledge of them is so intimate. At every point they must choose whom to follow—their own leader or strangers. What a following entails is demonstrated by the shepherd who gives his life for the sheep. The context of the analogy has thus been expanded, albeit with much violence to the simple metaphorical image, to include the total cast in the drama of salvation: God, Christ, their opponents, the thieves, Christ's undershepherds and their opponents the hirelings, the sheep and wolves, and the "other sheep that are not of this fold." The simple promise of Form A 3 has become quite complex. Yet once the community accepted Jesus as the speaker, with his followers as the audience and God as the one who opens the door, and once the fate of those who refused to knock was included, it became difficult to resist the impulse to add virtually every item in the Johannine allegory. John 10 shows what Christian imagination could do with a command-promise like Form A 3, as soon as the Passion Story had given its own shocking exegesis of how Jesus himself had knocked and entered that door.

(4) A different kind of imagination has given shape to the same command-promise in the Apocalypse, but there is still a recognizable kinship. John visualized the heavenly Son of man as holding the key of David, the keys to Death and Hades (1:18; 3:7). No one else could shut the door which he opened or open the door which he shut. All the choices facing the church at Philadelphia were defined by the fact that he had placed before them an open door (3:7, 8). That which separated heaven from earth was visualized as a door, so that the

gift of prophetic disclosure was described by the opening of that door (4:1). To enter the city by the gates was the highest conceivable good (22:14). The assurance that those gates would never be shut became therefore a powerful encouragement for men whose whole life could be characterized as knocking; but this did not erase the threat of exclusion against the "unclean" (21:25-27). Both promise and demand were symbolized by the twelve gates, each of which is cut through a single pearl. In this image one may discern the paradox of costly grace: each pearl is a gate big enough to serve as a wide and inviting entrance to the streets of gold, big enough to represent the population of this glorious city, the fulfillment of God's promise to the twelve tribes (21:12) together with the nations and their kings (21:24). Yet as a gate each single pearl is also narrow enough to require every entrant to sell all he has (Matt. 13:46) and to oblige him to choose a road so narrow that few can find it (Matt. 7:14). In Form A 3 the image of knocking readily came to represent for early Christians the difficulty of surviving the apocalyptic crisis, while the promise of an opened door came to represent their incredible confidence in Jesus' power over Death and Hades. In its context in Matt. 7:7, as interpreted by the parable of 7:9-11, the command to knock probably had lost some of this bright eschatological color, though as the word of a prophet of the kingdom of God it had originally glowed with such color. In this respect the prophet John in Revelation may be closer to the original meaning of the command than was the teacher in Matthew.

A 2—Seek, and You Will Find

This middle item in the triplex Form A suffers from its position. It was virtually overlooked in both the Matthean and Lukan contexts in spite of its congeniality with specific teachings in those contexts, e.g., Matt. 6:33. Yet few catchwords are more ubiquitous in both Testaments than the succinct combination of seeking and finding. The linguistic history of this formula is as long as the covenant history itself. The Law and the Prophets had long established the habit of thinking in which to seek is to seek God and his salvation. As instances:

The Law:	The Lord will scatter you among the peoples . . . and from there you will seek the Lord your God, and you will find him, if you search after him with all your heart and with all your soul. *(Deut. 4:27, 29.)*
The Prophets:	Seek the Lord while he may be found, call upon him while he is near. *(Isa. 55:6.)*
The Hymnbook:	Thou hast said, "Seek ye my face." My heart says to thee, "Thy face, Lord, do I seek." Hide not thy face from me. *(Ps. 27:8, 9.)*
The Proverbs:	I love those who love me, and those who seek me diligently find me. *(Prov. 8:17.)*

In the New Testament the collocation of finding/seeking has become axiomatic; it is applied to both trivial and ultimate matters. In the main, however, the object of seeking always represents an important concern: fruit (Luke 13:7), a lost coin (Luke 15:8), a lost sheep (Matt. 18:12), death (Rev. 9:6). Finding is by no means the automatic result of seeking (Mark 8:11). Yet seeking/finding has become a stereotype for the universal religious quest (Acts 17:27), while the refusal to seek spells sin and damnation (Rom. 3:11). As illuminating parallels to A 2, I shall select for examination three pericopes from among many passages.

(1) In Matthew the seeking/finding axis is central to the twin parables of the treasure hidden in a field and the merchant finding a pearl (13:44-46). Both are pictures of

obedience to the command "Seek first the kingdom of heaven" (6:33). The act of seeking is here viewed as the most important thing a man can do, while the treasure found is the greatest value a man can receive. The search as a whole is viewed as relating a man to the kingdom of heaven. These parables show how Matthew understood A 2 (cf. 7:14; 10:39; 11:29; 16:25). And it is probable, given the use of the axiom in the earlier period, that this understanding was also characteristic of those oral and written sources in which he found his materials.

(2) In rather striking contrast is the meditation in John on the conundrum which puzzled his audience, "You will seek me and you will not find me" (7:25-36). The whole chapter is a highly symbolic story of various quests by the Jews (7: 1, 4, 7, 11, 19, 25). Did the Jews really seek him, or was their seeking in reality a non-seeking? Why could they not find him? Where would he be—in the Dispersion or some other place? Over against their non-quest and its non-fulfillment, Jesus issued his own call: "If any one thirst, let him come to me and drink" (7:37). We need not penetrate all levels of meaning in the episode before making these observations: The use of the riddle in 7:34 presupposes the currency of a proverb like A 2 as background for the riddle itself. The ability to comprehend the proverb and the riddle is assumed to form the boundary line which separated Jews (7:35) from Christians. Thus seeking and finding *Jesus* has become the central clue to meaning. Seeking him has come to epitomize the total desiring of men, and finding him to epitomize their redemption.

(3) Another context which evokes quite different potential meanings in Form A 2 is provided by the Gospel of Thomas (#2, 92, 94) which is closely related to the Gospel of the Hebrews (Clem. Alex., Strom. V.14, 96, 3) and to Oxyrrhynchus Papyrus 654.1.

> He who seeks, let him not cease seeking until he finds;
> and when he finds he will be troubled,

> and if he is troubled he will be amazed,
> and he will reign over the All.[1]

Obviously this is a highly developed saying which has taken shape around such a nucleus as Form A 2. The development provides answers to some of the questions provoked by that command-promise. How long should a person seek? Until he finds. Does a person find exactly what he is looking for? No; otherwise he would not be troubled. What he finds is a knowledge which impels him to marvel (an esoteric gnosis as suggested by Logion 3). He also finds a power to reign over the All (a cosmological victory for the initiates) which includes deliverance from death (Logion 1). To whom is the command given? It was given secretly to Didymus Judas Thomas for him to disclose to selected individuals. The full understanding, however, would come only after long and arduous seeking. In this Gospel the accent falls upon the need for patient obedience to the command because of the esoteric nature of the objective sought.

The uses of the proverbial Form A 2 show how this saying could circulate quite independently of A 1 and A 3, also how provocative it was and how readily it could be adapted to varying situations. None of these alternate formulations was as simple, smooth, short, or memorable as A 2, a fact which supports its primitiveness. Yet all of them agree that the saying had a maximum relevance when the object of seeking was assumed to be men's salvation. Ideas of seeking were as variable as the ideas of salvation.

A 1—Ask, and It Will Be Given You

Anyone who sets out to trace the multiform history of this pithy saying embarks on a lifetime task. There are no limits to the forms it takes in the oral traditions of many peoples. To sketch a neat chart of its development, with the separate stages clearly arranged, is impossible. Nevertheless we may

[1] R. McL. Wilson, "The Gospel of Thomas," Saying 2, in *New Testament Apocrypha* I:511.

note recurring motifs in the New Testament, some of which are epitomized by A 1 and some of which are provoked by it.

We must first observe that these twin actions (asking and receiving, or asking and being given) appear often in the Old Testament. It is common to Semitic folklore that a sure mark of kingship is the ability to give whatever is asked. It is also the sign of special favor that a person receives such a pledge from the king (Mark 6:23). After God had given Israel a king in response to their request, he gave to Solomon an answer to his prayer (I Kings 3:5-14). The same relationship of asking and giving is a prime constituent of God's promise to his Anointed in Ps. 2:8, a text which had wide influence on early Christologies. The letters of Paul disclose many situations in the life of the first generation when the churches' dependence on God was articulated in terms of unceasing prayer. The command to ask was issued by the apostle on many occasions: "Let your requests be made known to God" (Phil. 4:6; Eph. 3:20). The promise of receiving certain gifts from God was no less frequent (Rom. 8:28-32; Phil. 4:19). The Lord "bestows his riches upon all who call upon him" (Rom. 10:12). Nowhere did Paul cite A 1, but his thought was permeated both by the urgency of the demand and by the reliability of the promise. Yet he saw no contradiction between this confidence and the refusal of God to grant things for which Paul had himself asked (II Cor. 12:7-9). Other writers were equally candid in recording requests which were not granted (Mark 10:35-36; 14:35). Three contexts selected for A 1 merit more extended treatment.

(1) In Mark the saying is placed as an immediate sequel to the devastation of the fig tree and as an explication of the command "Have faith in God" (11:20-24). "Whatever you ask in prayer, believe that you receive it, and you will." Faith is here defined by trust and confidence in God's goodness and power. Conversely, this *pistis* is explicitly declared to be a prior condition of the promise: "believe that you will receive." Moreover, that promise covers three types of request: the request for a mountain to be cast into the sea, the curse

on the fig tree, and the plea for forgiveness (vss. 14, 21, 23, 25). Although it is clearly stated that the request must be made "in prayer," these three examples show how many actions may be included within prayer. More important than prayer as the mode of asking is the warning that there must be no doubt "in the heart." The teaching is obviously older than this Markan context, but the context shows several aspects of Mark's interpretation of Form A 1, especially the hyperbolic character of the promise and the prerequisite of faith to activate the principle. It is perhaps instructive to ponder whether Mark saw connections between this command to believe in chap. 11 and the initial command of Jesus to believe in the good news (1:15).

(2) Interest in the relationship between asking and believing recurs in James, but with a varied accent. He stresses the amazing generosity of God toward all men (1:5) as the source of every perfect gift (1:17). He also develops the prerequisite of faith by insisting that doubting and double-mindedness cancel all hopes of receiving anything (1:6-8). In addition, he reflects at length on the character of the things which should be requested. What things can a person request with assurance that they will be granted? The first answer is "wisdom" (1:5), but excluded is a huge range of desires which can never be granted. "You ask and do not receive, because you ask wrongly, to spend it on your passions" (4:3). To seek what the world seeks is to become God's enemy, and no enemy can expect God to sustain him (4:4). Why does this author juxtapose the charge of not asking in 4:2 with the asking wrongly of 4:3? Are the two synonymous? If so, the validity of A 1 is maintained without serious amendment: "You do not have because you do not ask." This negative statement presupposes a knowledge of A 1 as a basic law and explains away its failures as only apparent. Those who make requests as enemies of God do not really ask; asking is genuine only when voiced by "the spirit which he has made to dwell in us" (4:5). James is an author whose mind begins with the positive promise of A 1 and

then deals with the difficulties which men had found in its operation.

(3) Nowhere does the teaching of A 1 become the occasion for more extensive reflection than in the Gospel and Epistle of John (John 4:10; 11:17-27; 14:1-17; 15:1-27; 16:20-33; I John 3:22, 24; 5:10-21). At times the discussion comes to a focus in a brief summary in which the minimal structure of A 1 provides the nucleus:

> If we ask (anything according to his will) he hears us.
> (And if we know that) he hears us in whatever we ask,
> (we know that) we have obtained the requests made of him.
> (*I John 5:14, 15.*)

> We receive from him whatever we ask. (*I John 3:22.*)

> Whatever you ask the Father in my name, he may give it to you.
> (*John 15:16.*)

> Ask, and you will receive, that your joy may be full.
> (*John 16:24.*)

What characterizes these passages is the fact that the brief axiomatic formulas of the earlier traditions have become the subject of highly involuted meditations. This has happened because those formulas were highly charged symbols of the internal relations which linked the disciples to the Son and the Father. "In my name" qualifies every valid request (14:14; 15:16); the same phrase qualifies the gift of God (16:23). In some passages it is the Son who fulfills the request (14:13), in others it is the Father (15:16; 16:23); but this difference is of no real moment because of their mutual indwelling (14:11). Both the command and the promise are predicated on the basis of Jesus' going to the Father (14:12), the advent of the Spirit (14:15-17), the call by Jesus (15:16), the love of the Father, and Jesus' victory over the world (16:25-33). It is assumed that God will grant whatever Jesus asks of him. So, for instance, when he who is the resurrection asks life for Lazarus, the request is immediately granted (11:22-26, 41-43). The dialogue with the Samaritan woman centers in the request and subsequent gift of water, as tantamount to the request and gift of eternal life (4:7-15). These Johannine meditations serve to answer various questions posed by Form A 1. To whom is the promise given? To those who believe in Christ, who keep his commandments, who love the Father and the brothers, who abide in the Son, and who are indwelt by the Spirit and inherit eternal life (I John 3:19-24; 5:13-15). For what kind of requests is the promise intended? The request must be made "according to his will" (I John 5:14) and in his name. A petition is valid when it requests "life for those whose sin is not mortal" (I John 5:16), or for eternal life for the petitioner, or for the power to do "greater works" (John 14:12), or for the bearing of much fruit (John 15:7, 8), or for the joy of Jesus (16:24). It is because of this prior relation between grantor and petitioner that there is a curious inversion of tenses: "If we know that he hears us in whatever we ask, we know that we *have obtained* the requests made of him" (I John 5:15. This discovery that one who prays has already been granted his petition was thought to be true of Jesus' own prayers, John 11:41). In a similar way the intercessions in the "high priestly prayer" are for those whom God has already given to Jesus. Jesus' present solidarity with them is both the substance of his request and the gift which he has already received from God (17:22-26).

One effect of this treatment of Form A 1 in the Eucharistic Discourses is this: the asking and the receiving come to encompass and to articulate all the bonds which, after the Passion, united the community to the Father, the Son, and the Spirit. The mutual indwelling of the divine and the human was visualized in such a way that men might know that their requests have already been granted before they are made, because the requests themselves are expressions of their life, their joy, and their faith as sons of the Father. The Johannine meditations are so complex and so full of thought that it is quite impossible to compress them into a set of conceptual boxes. Even so, they do make it entirely clear that the teaching of Form A 1 had generated an endless volume of profound reflections. These reflections had led Christian thinkers into very deep levels of spiritual introspection. This entire traditionary process can be understood only if Form A 1 was widely current as a central pivot of thought from the earliest days.

Summary

As we look back now and ponder all the strands of evidence concerning the three sayings in Form A, the basic impression is one of exuberant proliferation of thinking produced by this nuclear formula. So prolific is the undergrowth that any map becomes a questionable undertaking indeed. Nevertheless, let me hazard a few generalizations.

1. In most contexts the teacher is assumed to be Jesus, speaking in his role as teacher, prophet, and savior.
2. The command and promise are directed to the community which recognized his authority.
3. Both command and promise are understood as a dependable expression of God's will for his people.
4. The command and promise are taken to be especially relevant to the situation of prayer, but prayer is conceived as expressive of all the community's desires and needs.
5. The command and promise implicitly presuppose faith on the part of men and grace on the part of God, both faith and grace being considered in unlimited, hyperbolic fashion.
6. Men's objectives in asking, seeking, knocking are commonly assimilated to the "first" and "last" things: the approach of the kingdom of God, the gifts of eternal life and wisdom, which the coming of Jesus had represented.
7. God's grace in giving is commonly linked to God's salvation as a whole as announced by Jesus, rather than to specific human requests.
8. There is full recognition of the miraculous character

of the faith underlying the teaching. It is not viewed as an everyday prudential adage for all situations and all men, but as a teaching which spells out the conflict between the church and the world, or between the new age and the old.

9. Both the command and the promise are normally adapted to a community engaged in such tensions with outsiders that their requests are basic to survival and the promises of God are productive of such confidence and courage as are needed by martyrs.
10. Form A commands that its recipients invest themselves in their hope so fully that it comes to embody their total being; it supports this command so unconditionally as to ignore any danger of frustration, to exclude despair, and to override all tendencies in the direction of calculated caution. The very exorbitance of imagery is striking corroboration of the actuality of a transformed existence on the part of both the savior and the saved.
11. The wide currency of the command-promise in oral tradition, and therefore in the living memory of the community, made it an intimate part of the effectively incarnated scripture of that community from its beginning. The ease of memorization was matched by the frequency with which the substance of the command proved relevant to emergency needs. Wherever the prophet's word proved relevant, there the presence of the prophet himself would be manifested.
12. Although there are few direct textual links between this command and the Markan summary of Jesus' message in Mark 1:15, this command would be most at home in a community which had accepted the theology, eschatology, and Christology implicit in that message. This command, in turn, throws light on the various "structural girders" in that message (cf. above, pp. 24-25).

8 Be Carefree

He who fights the future has a dangerous enemy . . . .
Through the Eternal we can conquer the future.

Kierkegaard

The prohibition of anxiety was viewed throughout the early church as an important requirement prescribed by Jesus for all disciples without exception. Matthew signaled this importance by his inclusion of it in the Sermon (6:25-34). Luke accepted it as an essential guideline for the followers who were facing the eschatological crisis embodied in the situation of persecution (12:22-32). Its strategic importance is also reflected by the number and kind of accretions which the nuclear command attracted in oral tradition during the period of *ca.* A.D. 30-150. There are multiple versions of the command in second-century collections, e.g., the Gospel of Thomas, the Oxyrrhynchus Papyri, Justin Martyr, *et al.* Ever since, the inescapability and the impossibility of the demand have been recognized by successive generations of readers and preachers. In view of all this, it is rather curious that recent discussion among modern exegetes has been both limited and fragmentary. In his epoch-making *History of the Synoptic Tradition,* R. Bultmann gave only sporadic attention to several of the embedded proverbs.[1] F. W. Beare, following Bultmann, limited himself to a few generalities.[2]

[1] R. Bultmann, *The History of the Synoptic Tradition,* pp. 80-81, 103-7.
[2] F. W. Beare, *The Earliest Records of Jesus* (Nashville: Abingdon Press, 1962), pp. 62-64.

N. Perrin makes no reference to this passage in his *Rediscovering the Teaching of Jesus.* Although W. D. Davies devotes several hundred pages to *The Setting of the Sermon on the Mount,* he makes only passing reference to this teaching.[3] This neglect illustrates the fact that biblical exegesis, like many other activities, is subject to the sway of fashion. This paragraph throws far more light on Jesus' perspectives than recent study recognizes. At the same time it affords abundant evidence of various developments during the processes of transmission, stemming from particular situations and from shifting motivations in Christian usage. The following discussion is to provide ample evidence of these convictions.

Accretions in the Tradition

(25) Therefore I tell you, do not be anxious about your life, what you shall eat or what you shall drink, nor about your body, what you shall put on. Is not life more than food, and the body more than clothing? (26) Look at the birds of the air; they neither sow nor reap nor gather into barns, and yet your heavenly Father feeds them. Are you not of more value than they? (27) And which of you by being anxious can add one cubit to his span of life? (28) And why are you anxious about clothing? Consider the lilies of the field, how they grow; they neither toil nor spin; (29) yet I tell you, even Solomon in all his glory was not arrayed like one of these. (30) But if God so clothes the grass of the field, which today is alive and tomorrow is thrown into the oven, will he not much more clothe you, O men of little faith? (31) Therefore do not be anxious, saying, "What shall we eat?" or "What shall we drink?" or "What shall we wear?" (32) For the Gentiles seek all these things; and your heavenly Father knows that you need them all. (33) But seek first his kingdom and his righteousness, and all these things shall be yours as well. (34) Therefore do not be anxious about tomorrow, for tomorrow will be anxious for itself. Let the day's own trouble be sufficient for the day. (*Matt. 6:25-34.*)

Taking the Matthean version as a focus of study, a first step is to distinguish those elements which are nuclear from those which are accretions. Having sifted out the earliest

[3] W. D. Davies, *The Setting of the Sermon on the Mount* (New York: Cambridge University Press, 1964), pp. 300, 369, 381, 384, 458.

nuclei, we may then see whether we can reconstruct a credible sequence of developments in the form and function of the pericope.

It is likely that the brief introduction "Therefore I tell you" is pre-Matthean, for the identical Greek phrase is found in Luke and was therefore presumably present in Q. That both evangelists understood this *you* to refer to the inner band of disciples is clear. In Luke it is explicit (12:22*a*), in Matthew implicit (5:1). That they were correct in this understanding is suggested by several internal nuances. (1) The reference "your father" implies that the listeners have become sons, members of a new family circle (Matt. 6:26, 32; Luke 12:30). (2) An explicit contrast has been drawn to the behavior of outsiders, the Gentiles (Matt. 6:32; Luke 12:30). (3) The audience is made up of men who have been called to seek the Kingdom (Matt. 6:33; Luke 12:31). (4) In both Gospels these men are criticized because of their little confidence (*oligopistoi*), a characteristic way of rebuking disciples, not outsiders (Matt. 8:26; 14:31; 16:8; 17:20). (5) In Luke they constitute the "little flock" to whom God is pleased to give the Kingdom (12:32).

The identity and authority of the speaker is equally clear. The prohibition of anxiety for food and clothing presupposes a tendency toward anxiety for these things on the part of this particular audience; this in turn suggests that such anxiety may have been a by-product of loyalty to this particular speaker. In Matthew this teaching is preceded by the prohibition of earthly treasures and the requirement of unlimited almsgiving. In Luke it is prefaced by a prediction that disciples must endure trials before synagogues and kings, and by the parable of the rich fool; it is followed by the blunt command "Sell your possessions." Thus both evangelists provide contexts which give special force to the *therefore* (*dia touto*) of Matt. 6:25. Although these literary contexts are judiciously selected, neither was necessarily bound up with the transmission of the pericope and neither need be considered an original part of the teaching itself.

> Don't worry for food to sustain your life,
> or for clothing to cover your body.

This injunction is basic to the entire pericope. For one thing, it parallels exactly the two metaphorical and parabolic stanzas, the birds and the grass, the first of which illustrated the gathering of food, the second the weaving of cloth. It is an exact summary of the point of those parables. In both Matthew and Luke the prohibition is given twice, to introduce and to conclude the twin parables. The parables could have existed alone and the prohibition could have existed alone, but they fit together so naturally that it is well to consider them as designed at the outset to go together. This symmetry is destroyed, however, by the inclusion of drink in Matt. 6:25*b*, which most likely is secondary. Its addition was probably due to the popular tendency to associate drink with food as an essential of life. Followers of Jesus, however, had more certain access (as did birds and flowers) to water than to bread, and were far more likely to die from starvation than from thirst. The addition of drink adds nothing to the intrinsic thrust of the command.

> "Is not life more than meat, the body more than clothing?"

Although this question was attracted to the tradition about anxiety at a stage before Matthew and Luke edited that tradition, it cannot lay claim to being an intrinsic part of the original nucleus. The birds and flowers do not illustrate this distinction between life and food, between body and its raiment. Verse 25*a* says, "Don't worry about life," while 25*b* says, "Yes, you may well worry about life, but not about food." In short, the two halves of the same verse embody different uses of the basic terms *life* and *food.* They also reflect different reasons for avoiding worry. Verse 25*b* says not to worry about food, because it is relatively unimportant; 25*a* as interpreted by 25*b* therefore distorts the central command. It has little relevance to the distinctive vocation or risks of the disciplic community. It suggests that this community's evaluation of life and food should not depend on God's action or on Christ's mission or on the nearness of the Kingdom, but on a quite abstract analysis of comparative values. It assumes that men already have available the minimal requirements for survival, and that consequently they need not be concerned to secure excess food and clothing. The community is subjected less to the desperate fear of starvation than to the greed for more than the minimal essentials. We might say that the food in view in 25*b* is cake, not bread. Thus there is very little affinity between 25*b* and its adjoining passages. It seems to have been attracted to this location by nothing more than verbal assonance: life (*psyche*), body (*soma*), clothing (*endumatos*). It probably gravitated to this location later than did 25*a,* for as a question it could not easily introduce a command, even though its insertion broke the earlier sequence between 25*a* and 26. It is easier to imagine this interruption as having taken place during oral than during written transmission, though in either case it must be viewed as secondary.

Because the appeal to the birds originally matched the appeal to the lilies, those two metaphorical structures should be analyzed together. In both Gospels they are separated by an utterance that has no connection with either birds or grass, and little more connection with food and clothing:

> "Which of you by worry can add a single cubit to his stature?"

The very point of this interjection is the futility of worry, yet anxiety concerning food and clothing is not futile, or at least not necessarily so. Luke adds, "If you are unable to secure the least, why worry about other things?" The only connection between this saying and its neighbors is the negative attitude toward anxiety, as represented by the catchword *merimnan;* yet nowhere else is anxiety banned because of its futility. Such an appeal appears to be a pragmatic matter, based upon commonsense observation of how things go. Its cogency does not depend on a response to God's care, or Christ's summons, or the Kingdom's cost, or the behavior characteristic of disciples, or the risks accruing from faith. Its intrusion into the series of various sayings on anxiety appears to have occasioned two slight adjustments in Matthew: (1) Because it has broken the natural sequence from birds to grass, a new introduction to the latter is needed: "Why be anxious about clothing?" (2) The reference to the growth of the lilies (*pos auxanousin*) may have been occasioned by the reference to adding a cubit to one's height. "In neither a person's growth nor a plant's is the extent of growth proportional to the worry expended." This point, however effective it may be as an antidote to anxiety, obviously runs counter to the central concern in the twin parables.

That concern becomes clearer when we select the most symmetrical constituents and arrange them so that the symmetry is apparent, even though this entails rough treatment of the present text.

Don't worry about (a) food or (b) clothes:

a1 Look at the birds in the sky:
a2 They do not plant or thresh.
a3 Yet your heavenly Father feeds them.
a4 Are you not more valuable than they?

b1 Look at the lilies in the field.
b2 They do not work or weave.
b3 If God so clothes the hay in the field,
b4 will he not all the more clothe you?

In these lines we evidently find the nuclear saying around which the other teachings have gravitated during the transmissive process. Certainly there is nothing wooden about the parallelisms. Lines a 1 and b 1 are clear enough in their basic affinity. Lines a 2 and b 2 vary according to the two types of human activity required for securing food or clothes. Lines a 3 and b 3 establish as necessary premise the activity of God. Lines a 4 and b 4 raise rhetorical questions for which positive answers are required by that premise. To this conjectured skeletal structure we find in Matthew four minor emendations whose presence can be explained.

(1) The reference to how the lilies grow (vs. 28) provides

a subtle parallel to the growth in stature of man (vs. 27) but adds nothing to the force of the parable insofar as it stresses God's care for the survival of the disciples.

(2) The contrast between the glory of Solomon and the glory of the field flowers (vs. 29) strengthens the logic of the twin parables. The lilies' freedom from anxiety is not due to their plain and drab clothing; the more beautiful their appearance, the more amazing their lack of concern over clothing. Their beauty is an impressive token of God's care. Thus the "how much more" becomes in effect: "If God gives so much glory to grass, how much more gloriously will he clothe you."

(3) A more sombre note enters with the reference to the frailty of grass (cf. Isa. 40:6-7 LXX). The more beautiful the daisies or dandelions, the more pathetic their fragility and their cheapness. Here today, gone tomorrow. More glorious than Solomon, they are in the end useful only to feed the household fire. The former note sounds romantic; this one restores realism. It is indeed ominous evidence of God's care that the grass is so quickly reduced to ash. The first stanza would convey the same note if it mentioned the sparrow's cheapness and death, as in fact is done in Matt. 10:29-31. Does this strengthen the prohibition "be not anxious"? For most people, Isaiah's comparison of all flesh to grass is productive of anxiety. If, however, this teaching was addressed to a poor, persecuted minority who faced death as a daily hazard, this element in the poetic stanza would underscore the authenticity of the command, for the commander himself had been crucified. He had laid his cross on every follower. The burning of the grass would correspond figuratively to their shared expendability; yet by the same token it would reenforce his command. For them the "how much more" was uttered by one who knew all about the death of grass and men.

(4) The fourth addition in the second stanza is the word of address: "You whose confidence is weak" (*oligopistoi*). This makes clear that the occasion for the nuclear teaching was the anxiety, the fear, the dread, the despair on the part of Jesus' disciples as they calculated the prospects of their own survival. They had a controversy with God: "Why hast

thou forsaken us?" They seemed unable to secure their own food and clothing, the irreducible minimum of life's essentials. Actually this context provides a luminous definition of great faith or little faith in terms of the degree of trust in God's care. The mention of the furnace fires underscores both the difficulty and the necessity of such trust. It is likely that the image of the furnace (*klibanos*) connoted simultaneously the fires of persecution and those of final judgment (Hos. 7:4; I Peter 1:7; II Clem. 16:3). In this teaching Jesus speaks to followers who were standing at the junction between "little faith" and strong faith in God's grace; he was seeking to draw them into making a difficult decision.

In Matt. 6:31 the prohibition is repeated. This can therefore be treated as the logical conclusion of the birds/grass analogy. It may also be treated as the introduction to a somewhat separate teaching. The interest shifts subtly from the essentials for survival to a more generalized need for "all these things" (*panta tauta* is triply accented, in Matt. 6:32*a*, *b*, 33). In Luke 12, the concern is not primarily with the destitution which occasions anxiety, but with the direction of desires (*zeteite* becomes a verbal link between vss. 29, 30, 31). This recurrent stress on seeking calls attention to quite extensive parallelisms, both synonymous and antithetical, in the subsequent thought:

> Don't *seek* these things.
> For the Gentiles *seek* them.
> But *seek* the Kingdom,
> and these things will be added.
> For God knows your need.

These lines may show a paraenetic complex which originally was independent of the twin parables. At least we must notice different motivations. For one thing, the motive in Matt. 6:32 ceases to be that of countering anxiety and becomes one of separating oneself from the Gentiles. The objects of Gentile desires are unworthy to serve as objects of Christian desires. The fact that food and clothes are now viewed as secondary collides with the meaning of 26*c* and 30*c*. The desire to be superior to the Gentiles reflects an ecclesiastical situation dominated by non-eschatological and catechetical perspectives (cf. 5:47; 6:7; 18:17), factors which mark this Gentile appeal as secondary. If this appeal is primary it is because it serves as antithesis to vs. 33*a:* "The Gentiles seek these things; you must seek God's Kingdom." In this case the seeking of the Kingdom itself is viewed as defining the boundary between Israel and the Gentiles. In this case also the motivation remains distinct from that of the birds/grass metaphor. The problem of anxiety has been replaced by the question of the priority of desires. The concern with the priority among wants displaces the concern with either-or choices between two treasures and two masters, as in Matt. 6:19-24. The command to seek God's Kingdom thus appears to be the nucleus of this new series of sayings in 6:31-33. As the primary logion here, it probably originated in a situation separate from that of the birds/grass parables, and therefore it deserves separate treatment.

> vs.34*a* Don't be anxious about tomorrow,
> for tomorrow will be anxious about itself.

This proverb is obviously independent of its neighbors. It is a tiny chiasmus, perfect in form and balance. It is a secular aphorism that draws upon common sense and apparently has no necessary or logical connections with the distinctive elements in Christian faith or hope. The central problem is no longer that of food and clothes, but that of fretting about the future. In all likelihood it was coincidence of sound, i.e., the use of the verb *merimnan,* which attracted the saying to this location. Although there is no evidence of its presence in Q, neither is there any evidence of special Matthean interest in it. Its marginal character should be obvious.

> vs.34*b* Each day has enough trouble of its own.

This may have originally been a separate axiom, reflecting a rather grim attitude toward the present. If so, it was attracted to this series of teachings by the today-tomorrow contrast of 34*a*. It embodies a wry pragmatic wisdom concerning the human situation. It quite directly contradicts the "faith" which is illustrated by the birds and the grass, and becomes a matchless example of unfaith. If one obeyed its implied command, he would worry about today's evils, which are bad enough to keep him fully occupied. As such, this teaching is the polar opposite of Luke 12:32 and is almost as fully incompatible with the prohibition of Matt. 6:25*a*. It is curious, indeed, to find such cynicism within the Sermon on the Mount.

We have thus identified as the earliest nuclei of this cycle of sayings the twin parables of the birds and the grass (6: 25*a*, 26, 28*b*-30) and, less certainly, the command to seek the Kingdom (33*a*). Almost all the other items in the cycle can be explained as accretions during the process of oral transmission. Only a few details can be safely assigned to the editorial hand of Matthew: three additions (the phrase "heavenly father," the phrase "and its (or his) righteousness," the adverb "first") and possibly the omission of Luke 12:26. None of these redactional elements, apart from Matt. 6:27 and 6:34, seriously undermines the force of the nucleus. The profusion of various notions may obscure the simple radicalism of the parables, but there is no evidence of intentional corruption of meaning. We may well turn now to a closer scrutiny of the nucleus.

The Nucleus

You faithless disciples:
a Don't worry for food to sustain your life.
b (Don't worry) for clothes to cover your body.

a1 Look at the birds in the sky.
a2 They do not plant or thresh (or store in barns),
a3 yet your heavenly father feeds them.
a4 Are you not more valuable than they?

b1 Learn from the lilies in the field (how they grow).
b2 They do not work or weave
(In his royal garments Solomon was not so well dressed).

b3 If God so clothes the hay in the field
(which is here today but consumed in the oven tomorrow),
b4 Will he not all the more clothe you?

When compared to the other teachings in the paragraph, this twin analogy is to be seen as the longest continuous thread of thought. It is also the most complex in structure. The parallelisms are too extensive to be accidental. With an amazing economy of phrasing, the situation of the birds and the flowers is depicted. The style is highly picturesque and imaginative, though the idiom is unsophisticated and pastoral. The choice of imagery invites reflection and self-examination. (Many of Kierkegaard's most extensive meditations are stimulated by the parabolic richness of implication within these parables.) The modes of thinking are fully indigenous to a mind saturated with the Hebrew scriptures and an imagination kindled by the environment of Galilee.

The identity of speaker and audience is quite clearly implied by the parables. The teller is one who claims to know God's will. The listeners are his followers, viewed as the sons of God. They live under conditions in which anxiety about survival has developed, and they have succumbed to that anxiety. Their faith in God and in his promises has not yet proved strong enough to overcome it. Anxiety therefore threatens the fulfillment of God's purpose for them. Hence Jesus, whom they have chosen to follow, must issue an urgent rebuke, along with a prohibition against such worries. He sees a similarity between their situation and that of the birds/grass which they do not yet see, a similarity which he thinks may counter their fears, inasmuch as this similarity calls attention to God's care for them. In certain respects they are like grass, in other respects unlike. Jesus wants them to see both aspects.

It is important, I think, to recognize both the strength of their fears and the apparent implausibility of the analogy. For men facing death from starvation, how much confidence can be distilled from the security of sparrows? It was by no means true that birds always got enough to eat, that they led a charmed existence or were assured a long life. On the contrary, in proverbial lore they were symbols of helplessness, of transience, of cheapness (two were sold for a penny, Matt. 10:29). A prudent man would hardly select them as examples of security and longevity. They were beautiful, perhaps, but hardly convincing as examples of an assured future. Nor is there any greater assurance in the example of the grass which may be as beautiful as the birds, but is even less valuable and enduring. From a pragmatic standpoint it was folly to appeal to such objects as antidotes to anxiety. Why, then, should such an appeal be made? Surely it would not be made apart from the conviction that God cares for the birds and the grass. For one who wishes to emphasize God's care, the choice of objects so ephemeral (in the literal sense ἐφ-ἡμέρα) would serve to carry the point better than would lions or oak trees. Even so, the use of birds and grass to make this point should alert us to the folly which is taught in the twin parables. In looking, then, for situations in the early church in which this nuclear command would have a maximum relevance, we need to look for situations where Christians seemed to be as helpless and as short-lived as the birds and the grass, yet where their greater value in the sight of God could be affirmed. What situations were current in which Christians were simultaneously highly vulnerable in the sight of men, valuable in the sight of God, and hence under special difficulty and obligation to manifest their faith? If we can locate such situations we will discover the areas where this shocking teaching would have been thoroughly indigenous.

A first setting is suggested by Matt. 10, where the nearest parallel to the parable of the birds is found. There it is related to the special occupational hazards faced by the twelve apostles as they were sent to the cities of Israel, like sheep in the midst of wolves. Their lives would be those of penniless mendicants, dependent for the day's food on anonymous hosts (10:9-11). They could take no food with them and only enough clothing for the trip itself. They would be hated, betrayed, delivered up to death in a vocation like that of their master (10:21-25). Their fearlessness in face of persecution would become the measure of their freedom from anxiety (6:25-34). In fact, the paradox of the sparrow that does not die apart from God's will was matched by the numbering of the hairs on the head of the martyrs (10:28-31). We find the same paradox of complete trust in the face of desperate need in the only letters which come direct from one of the apostles who claimed to know "the secret of facing plenty and hunger, abundance and want" (Phil. 4:12). To him hunger was one of the means of commending his apostleship, along with the poverty which made many rich (II Cor. 6:4-10). It is not difficult to see how apostles like Paul would have cherished, from the Risen Lord, such prohibitions of anxiety as are found in Matt. 6:25-34.

Like apostle, like convert. The apostles called men to join a minority which faced similar dangers. The second potential setting, then, is provided by the demands laid on all Christians. Hunger and nakedness were more than metaphorical descriptions of the derelictions to which they were liable. Since fear was fused with these hazards, they could maintain faith only by overcoming fear. Each class of catechumens had to be prepared to battle with basic anxieties. It could not be otherwise when persecution was the price of membership in the Kingdom (Matt. 5:10, 11). Central to the catechesis was instruction in the ways of dealing with hunger and nakedness on the part of brothers (Matt. 25:35-45) as well as of oneself. The pithy injunction in I Peter is entirely typical of the training of converts: "Cast all your anxieties on him [God], for he cares about you" (5:7). It is not inappropriate, therefore, to allocate the birds/grass analogy to the typical catechetical tradition of the church from its earliest days on.

A third setting in which this analogy fits smoothly is provided by the practice of unlimited almsgiving. As we have seen, the command "give to everyone who asks" is firmly anchored in the primitive teaching (Matt. 5:42). If bread is asked, bread should be given; if a person's coat is requested, his shirt should accompany it. It is germane to call attention to the fact that to engage in such practices would make people increasingly vulnerable to anxiety. Presumably Ananias and Sapphira illustrate the peculiar prevalence of such worries in a community where, at least in idealized retrospect, all members "had all things in common" (Acts 2:43-47; 5:1-11). Presumably Luke saw these connections, for he inserted the pericope on anxiety between the account of a fool, whose desire to lay up treasure for himself prevented his becoming "rich toward God" (12:21), and the command to amass an assured treasure in heaven by giving alms (12:33).

All three of these settings belong within the eschatological perspective in which the kingdom of God has become so near that entrance into that Kingdom is viewed as being worthy of every sacrifice. A person is well advised to sell everything in order to buy the field in which the pearl is hidden. Heavenly and earthly treasure are set over against each other; a man cannot simultaneously seek or hope to gain both. For those seeking to serve God, it is enough to pray for bread for each day as it comes (Matt. 6:11). The fading of the flower becomes a token of the fading of the rich man "in the midst of his pursuits" (Jas. 1:10, 11). The well-known passage from Isaiah is primarily a reminder of the abiding power of God's word over against the transiency of grass (I Peter 1:24). For those awaiting the return of the Lord, freedom from anxiety for the things of this age serves as one measure of their alertness (Luke 12:35-38). In fact, the powerful conclusion of the birds/grass parable ("Are you not of more value than they?" "Will he not much more clothe you?") may have made sense only in view of the promise of abundant food and white clothes in the kingdom of God. An equivalent way of overcoming anxiety about food and clothes is the command in Luke, "Fear not, little flock, for it is your father's good pleasure to give you the Kingdom."

In this connection one should recall the multiple eschatological nuances in the image of food: e.g., the manna, the bread of heaven, the bread of life, the feeding of the multitudes, the Eucharist as a memorial of the Last Supper and as a foretaste of the messianic banquet. The image of clothing should recall the cognate notions of the shame of nakedness, the transfiguration of the body, the white clothes of holy men, the armor of light, the doffing of the old and donning of the "new man." In fact, the birds/grass analogy suggests one element in the expectation that the coming consummation would constitute a return to the pre-Fall paradise. Just as there had been a time before man had needed to till the ground for food or to find clothes to cover the shame of his nakedness, so now the fearlessness of those who lived at the dawn of the new day symbolized their participation in the plenty and security of life under the restored lordship of God.

In these four settings the teaching is fully indigenous. Are there any clues which would enable us to select one of these settings as the most appropriate or original? It is difficult to isolate such clues. Rather, the absence of such particularized indications of the *Sitz-im-Leben* underscores its affinity to all four. This effectiveness in so many contexts, all of which belong within the earliest period in the life of the church, substantiates the claim that the earliest provenance of this teaching belongs to the ministry of Jesus and to the earliest days in the church's experience of discipleship to him.

Among recent interpreters who have assigned a later and more specialized setting to this pericope the most noteworthy is W. D. Davies.[4] He suggests that this teaching reflects Matthew's reaction to the realism of the scribal school at Jamnia. Such freedom from anxiety as is commanded is characteristic of the enthusiastic and radical irresponsibility of the Galilean Christians, an attitude which Matthew defended against the cautious concern for food and clothing of the scribal school. Professor Davies' suggestion is far from convincing. It assumes that the issue at stake is the choice between two religious parties, one characterized by enthusiasm and the other by sober prudence. Is this really the issue? Rather, the actual option facing each Christian is whether or not he is to worry about his own survival. The solution of that problem depends on how much God could be counted on to care for this particular band of persecuted followers of Jesus. Although I am not convinced by it, Davies' interpretation has this to be

[4] *Ibid.*, pp. 300-301.

said in its favor: it rejects a tendency to view the birds/grass parables as an example of generalized wisdom teaching, a tendency illustrated in the following comment: "Jesus speaks as a teacher of Wisdom. . . . [These teachings] reflect . . . nothing that rises above the level of the wise saws that are found in all societies, the common-places of popular proverbs and copy-book maxims."[5] Such a judgment may apply to some of the secondary accretions (Matt. 6:25*c*, 27, 34); but to build up a sense of human security on the basis of God's care for sparrows is hardly an appeal to pragmatic common sense. The teaching only begins to get a grip on the listener's heart when as a result of his quest for the kingdom of God his life appears to be no more secure than the sparrow's. This is hardly the generalized situation which spawns prudential platitudes.

Hermeneutical Implications

Let us assume that our conclusions are correct: that the prohibition of anxiety supported by the twin parables constitutes the earliest recoverable nucleus in the tradition. Let us also assume that this nucleus comes from the earliest strata of the teaching tradition, from commands of Jesus issued during his ministry which, because of their peculiar relevance to continuing stress, were preserved after his death by Galilean disciples. Now two questions remain: with what other early teachings do they show such affinity that each helps to interpret the others? What theological stance seems to be reflected by this teaching when viewed in this context?

(1) We may first note the high degree of affinity to the other teachings in the Sermon on the Mount. The community addressed by the twin parables would find the Lord's Prayer entirely congenial: its address, its primary concern for God's Kingdom and the doing of God's will, its dependence on God for daily bread, its awareness of constant temptation by the devil. This community was commanded to invest all its securi-

[5] F. W. Beare, *The Earliest Records of Jesus*, p. 63.

ties in heaven (Matt. 6:19-21) and to allow the divine verdict to displace human judgments of piety and security (6:1-18; 7:1-5). It was called to fearlessness of men and total trust in God's care (7:7-11), although the difficulty of such trust made them constantly aware of the narrowness of the gate (7:13, 14). The beatitudes breathe the same paradoxical blessedness in the midst of hunger and poverty for those whose sufferings were transmuted into joy (5:3-12). Simple trust like that of sparrows and grass enabled this community to give without stint to every beggar and to pray for every persecutor (5:38-48). In fact, the confidence in a God whose sun shines on evil and good alike is precisely the same confidence as that recommended by the falling sparrow.

The radicalism of the no-anxiety clause was most intelligible among men who viewed the loss of life as its gain (Matt. 10:39; 16:24-26). It made most sense where "the cares of this world" were recognized as enemies of the Word (Matt. 13:22), where concerns for survival were seen as equivalent to "drunkenness and sleep" (Luke 21:34). In such a community the stories of the multitudes in the wilderness, being fed by Jesus, carried maximum appeal. It was not surprising to them to visualize the Judge of all men saying, "I was hungry . . . , I was naked . . ." (Matt. 25:42-45). To be sure, such a community found it difficult to obey Christ's command; otherwise there would have been no need to reiterate it. Yet these same men accepted the authority of Jesus to issue such orders, along with the authority of his apostles to make them binding. For example:

> Have no anxiety about anything, but in everything by prayer and supplication with thanksgiving let your requests be made known to God. *(Phil. 4:6.)*

(2) The preceding survey of congenial teachings makes it easier to answer our next question: what theological attitudes are reflected by the twin parables, when those parables have been placed back into the four types of situation we have outlined? The attitude toward God is expressed most clearly in the Matthean "your heavenly Father" (6:26; in Luke 12:24,

God). The teaching defines fatherhood in terms of the value to him of his sons, in terms of his care for them as comparable to his care for birds and grass. This concern is assumed to reach throughout the whole of creation, of which birds and grass are very modest representatives. More than concern is involved, for it is assumed also that God knows what every creature needs and that he has the full power to provide it. Thus the parables artlessly and gracefully assume what later systematicians were to classify as God's omniscience, his omnipresence, and his omnipotence, all these attributes being subsumed under the assurance of his care for an ordinary sparrow.

If, as we have insisted, the parables fully recognized the cheapness, the brevity, and the unimportance of the birds and the grass, they simultaneously indicated a recognition that God's power and care are belied by appearance. God reverses all earthly measurements of permanence and of value. His concern for his creatures is hidden from the casual eye. There is a mystery surrounding his treatment of sparrows and of sons, and this mystery comes to a focus in the ways in which he fulfills his promises to those whose fate is comparable to that of the grass (Matt. 6:30). The mystery of God's care is the mystery of the unique life which is bestowed by him in his Kingdom, the mystery of a treasure laid up in heaven for those whose hearts are there (6:19-21), a treasure which provides them with ample food and clothing. Although this reference to the Kingdom is not included within the twin parables, the tradition in both Matthew and Luke was surely right in combining the parables with explicit allusions to the Kingdom. The image of the dawning Kingdom was the conceptual form taken by the confidence, courage, hope, and love for God which became operative whenever the community obeyed these stringent orders of their master.

A moment's reflection will also support the observation that the implicit theology and eschatology are accompanied by a Christology. Who is this man who claims to have such dependable knowledge of God's will and ways? How did such knowledge come to him? By a prophetic vision of heaven? Who is it who asserts so naturally the right to set such an unqualified requirement for all members of his community? How was such authority conferred? Who is it whose word this group accepts without debate as bearing the highest authority? What has he done to earn the right to treat so lightly the normal human passion for survival? If his audience constitutes a family of God's sons, who is he? A son, an emissary of the father, or both? Obedience to his command "Be not anxious" contains within itself the implicit answers to such questions as these. Every teacher who transmitted these teachings, before and after Matthew, took those answers for granted.

No less than Christology, a specific ecclesiology is also embedded in these parables. They convey a definition of faith within a community characterized by "little faith," so that this church might in fact become the Church. They have become sons of the same father and therefore mutually dependent on one another as "the flock" of a well-known shepherd. If "the grass" is more glorious than Solomon and they are more precious to God than the grass, how great the glory in their very existence, even though that existence be as uncertain as that of the grass. Their new relationship of total confidence in a gracious God, their new security as heirs of God's Kingdom, their new freedom from fear as they face a stubbornly hostile world—all this had been made possible by the advent among them of a teacher and his disciple-apostles. The skeletal structure of the church is thus present in the form of this parabolic imperative. To obey it was to accept this community as defining the selfhood of each member in his thinking about such essentials as bread and clothes. Anxiety could be overcome only if men responded to the announcement that the time was fulfilled by obeying the command to repent and to trust (Mark 1:15). To obey was to confess that the heart's treasure was in fact invested in a communal goal that transcended the "cares of this world." But this confession remained free of romantic perversion, because God's care for his sons was known to be supremely manifested in the hunger and nakedness of his only son. There was nothing idyllic in the life either of the one who prohibited anxiety or of the community which preserved his prohibition and tried with varying degrees of success to obey it. Yet the very substance of salvation, i.e., existence under the Kingdom's power, was promised "in, with, and under" such obedience.

9 Watch and Pray

To awaken the sleeping and rouse the loitering is a work of supreme mercy.

Unamuno,
Perplexities and Paradoxes

According to all three Synoptics, Jesus commanded his followers to watch. Various verbs are used: *gregorein, blepein, agrupnein.* In this study we will concentrate on the first. In the Epistles this command remained current and viable as a standard element in Christian teaching. Among the demands which were resonant in the ears of the first generation, however, few ring so hollow in modern ears. Relevance appears to be confined to the period when apocalyptic expectations were at their height or when leaders of the churches, confronted with unforeseen delays in the Parousia, sought to fan the cooling ardor of their followers. In spite of this apparent irrelevance, it will be worth our while to examine early uses of this command. This study must follow a somewhat different path from the study of such pericopes as Matt. 6:25-33, or 7:7-11, because here we are not dealing with a highly cohesive unit of oral tradition in which separate stages of development may be laid bare. In this case the continuing nucleus is the single word *gregorein,* the force of which derives from the varying historical or parabolic contexts which come down to us in specific literary traditions. In this respect this command is similar to the command to repent. Accordingly we will concentrate not upon distinguishing the nucleus from its successive oral accretions, but upon meanings imparted to the command by the varying literary contexts.

In our exegesis we begin by recognizing the fact that, although the issuing of the command is clear enough, there is an almost unlimited ambiguity in the kinds of action which may embody obedience to it. It is this area of vagueness which we will seek to diminish. What specific attitudes, actions, or behavior patterns does this command seek to elicit? By what visible or tangible marks is a watchful man separated from a sleepy man—for watching and sleeping are everywhere assumed to be opposites? A thousand other questions are spun off by this demand, but this single one will absorb our attention.

Mark 13:33-37

Take heed, watch; for you do not know when the time will come. It is like a man going on a journey, when he leaves home and puts his servants in charge, each with his work, and commands the doorkeeper to be on the watch. Watch therefore—for you do not know when the master of the house will come, in the evening, or at midnight, or at cockcrow, or in the morning—lest he come suddenly and find you asleep. And what I say to you I say to all: Watch.

Many scholars have underscored the importance of the location of this parable in the theological topography of Mark. Virtually all interpreters have stressed the fact that this Gospel concentrates attention upon the Passion Story, which Mark introduced as early as 11:1 with his account of the entry into Jerusalem. The placing of the misnamed "Little Apocalypse" (13:3-37) within the Passion Story, between the temple controversies and the Last Supper, was far from accidental or peripheral to Mark's purpose. Jesus' final address to his disciples was symbolically staged "on the Mount of Olives opposite the temple." This location brings into play many of the nuances of the term mountain (ὄρος) in early Christian thought. More particularly, it reminds us that the Messiah was expected to appear on this very mountain (Zech. 14:4), an expectation of which Mark was probably aware.

Nor should we overlook the dramatic timing of this address between the decision to arrest Jesus and that event itself. It is the immediate sequel to the conflict with Israel's leaders and the prophecy of the temple's destruction; it is the immediate prelude to the anointing, the betrayal, and the covenanted meal. A clear sign of its importance is the twin fact that the audience is limited to the four representatives of the Twelve, and yet that this audience is widened in vs. 37 to "all." So much for the dramatic centrality of the address as a whole.

Even more important for our purpose is the climactic location within the chapter of the parable in vss. 33-37. The function of the chapter is to underscore the relevance of this paragraph; the function of this paragraph, in turn, is to underscore the command, which is repeated three times. It is this very command which is made obligatory on the four, the twelve, and finally the "all"—three concentric circles in Mark's conception of the audience of Jesus.[1] To say this, however, does not carry us far toward our goal. It stresses the significance of the command, but it does not diminish the vagueness of its content. To achieve that goal we must examine the literary context more closely.

Does the thought of vss. 33-37 conclude the series of answers to the question raised in vs. 4, "when will this be . . . ?" If so, the command to watch parallels a number of cognate warnings (vss. 5, 9, 11, 14, 23). Does the command fit most neatly within the situations of trials and beatings described in vss. 9-11? Or is the command to watch occasioned by the rise of false prophets with their deceptive marvels (vs. 22)? It is clearly applied to men who see "these things" (vs. 29) taking place, but what those things actually are is a matter that remains undefined. Everything that is mentioned in the chapter might be included. It is obvious that the imperative could have been prompted by many different crises, a fact which makes it relatively separate from any one crisis in particular. Its relevance is not limited to a narrow range of nonrecurrent

[1] Cf. my essay "Audience Criticism and Markan Ecclesiology," in *Neues Testament und Geschichte.*

emergencies. Readers may assume that the entire cycle of sayings in vss. 3-32, being more determinable, should define the meaning of vss. 33-37. They may, on the contrary, assume that the concluding paragraph should control the exegesis of the highly enigmatic collage of earlier sayings. In either case we have not moved much nearer to our goal of defining what kind of actions constitute obedience to the demand to watch. For this we must look for clues to the pericope itself.

For instance, the saying visualizes a period between the departure and the return of a lord, a period when the faithfulness of servants is being subjected to testing. One coordinate of watchfulness is the knowledge that the event will take place within a generation (vs. 30). Watching appears to be an embodiment of this knowledge. Yet it is also an embodiment of the fact that the watchers cannot know the day or the hour (vss. 32, 33, 35). It is this ignorance which impels them to watch. The analogy of the fig tree better connotes the knowledge of the nearness of summer; the picture of the returning lord more aptly connotes the ignorance of the precise time. The two analogies may thus contradict each other, but if they do, Mark was quite unaware of it. Whatever decision watchfulness entailed, it was visualized as an action appropriate to nighttime. The four periods itemized in vs. 35 are the four watches of the night, normally distinguished in ordinary Roman reckoning. If the term "night" is used symbolically, then the act of watching also becomes symbolic. Of that we can be quite sure. If the time scale is the night and if this night represents the present evil age in its demonic, transient, and deceptive character, watching must connote those kinds of attitude and action which are characteristic of men who resist the temptations of this age because of their loyalty to their absent lord.[2]

The parable of vs. 34 does more, however, than define the time scale. It also defines the end of the period, and therefore the event which absorbs the watcher's attention. Just as

[2] Cf. Evald Lövestam, *Spiritual Wakefulness in the New Testament* (Lund: University of Lund Press, 1963), p. 135.

vs. 29 defines the time of harvest by the arrival of a man at the doors, so vs. 35 defines the *kairos* as the arrival of the returning lord. There is even a strong convergence between these two definitions in the verbal link between "door" (*thura*) in vs. 29 and "doorkeeper" (*thuroros*) in vs. 34. The doorkeeper watches for the One who stands at the door. It is surely the latter who determines which actions of the former constitute waking or sleeping. The character of those actions is further clarified by the parable. They must be in harmony with the work (*ergon*) which this lord has assigned to each; there must be a faithful use of his delegated authority (*exousia*). This work and this authority stamp them as his servants. The parable twice labels them "his house" (vss. 34, 35), a term which in Mark's day often connoted the church. The parable draws a distinction between the gatekeepers and the other servants, with the work of watching assigned to the former. This corresponds to the distinction between leaders and laymen in the early church. The former shared authority with the others, though they had a special assignment within the household.

Although the parable in vs. 34 thus provides the primary clues to the meaning of the command, the parable cannot stand by itself as an independent unit of tradition. It is incomplete and entirely dependent on what precedes it. This dependence is indicated by the conjunction "as" (*hos*). Verse 33 is address in the second person, vs. 35 returns to that address. The parable is third person throughout. In vss. 33 and 35 it is the lord who commands his servants to watch. In vs. 34 it is a parable *about* the lord by some nameless speaker. Yet every nuance and word of the parable is indigenous to the ethos of the Markan church. Within that ethos the parable becomes wholly intelligible. The use of the church's vocabulary inevitably turned the incomplete parable into an extensive allegory, each word of which evoked multiple connotations in Christian imaginations. Clearly Mark and his readers were already familiar with the allegorical code; in fact, allegorical ways of visualizing the current situation comprised the mother tongue of this community.[3] Within the boundaries of that linguistic world, the command to watch could conjure up pictures of an army sentinel, a shepherd guarding his flock, friends of the bridegroom, a householder guarding his home against thieves, and stewards charged with feeding a large family. The metaphorical situations were more varied than the command, a fact which proves that the same command was applicable to many different situations and actions. Even more constant than the command, however, was the fact that all the metaphorical elements gravitated around the axis of the lord's dealing with his servants. It seems to be this relationship which becomes verbalized in the command *gregorein.* This may explain why there are so many ambiguities in the time and place and mode of watching, and why the act itself could not be codified or objectified. The significance of the word and the action depended upon translating the Christian's actual situation into the language of the parable: "It is like a man going. . . ." As we look at other occasions for the same demand, we will test the cogency of these preliminary observations.

Mark 14:32-42

And they went to a place which was called Gethsemane; and he said to his disciples, "Sit here, while I pray." And he took with him Peter and James and John, and began to be greatly distressed and troubled. And he said to them, "My soul is very sorrowful, even to death; remain here, and watch." . . . And he came and found them sleeping, and he said to Peter, "Simon, are you asleep? Could you not watch one hour? Watch and pray that you may not enter into temptation; the spirit indeed is willing, but the flesh is weak."

The demand recurs almost immediately in the Gethsemane account (Mark 14:32-42), the only other passage where Mark uses the word *gregorein.* In fact, in each of these two passages the word appears three times, a frequency which is hardly

[3] The situation with its imperatives produced the analogy; therefore the boundaries between the literary forms of parable and allegory become very vague. Cf. R. E. Brown in *Novum Testamentum* 5 (1962): 38; E. Lövestam, *Spiritual Wakefulness in the New Testament,* p. 90.

accidental. In both, the dialogue occurs on the Mount of Olives between the Lord and selected representatives of the Twelve. This location is highly significant, since it not only links the farewell address of chap. 13 to its fulfillment in Gethsemane (14:32-42), but it treats both events as fulfillments of the prophecy of Zech. 13:6–14:7. Here take place the predicted striking of the shepherd, his receiving of wounds in the house of his friends, the scattering of the sheep, the testing of God's little ones "as gold is tested," the coming of the day of the Lord at "evening time" (14:1-7), when "his feet shall stand" on the Mount of Olives. Reference to that mountain in Mark 13:3 and in 14:26 is the equivalent of a section heading intended to cover the stories which follow, at least to the end of chap. 14.[4] Since the Gethsemane story was the intended sequel to the parable in 13:33-37, that story must be treated as the earliest exegesis of the parable. We must examine the evidence for such connections.

Two British scholars have presented persuasive summaries of that evidence. R. H. Lightfoot[5] discovered a number of parallels "between the apocalyptic prophecy (Ch. 13) and the Passion Narrative (Ch. 14, 15)" (p. 51). For example there is a significant continuity in the use of the verb *to deliver up* (παραδίδοναι), which in chap. 13 applies three times to the sufferings of the disciples (13:9, 11, 12) and in chaps. 14, 15 ten times to the sufferings of their Lord (14:10, 11, 18, 21, 41, 42, 44; 15:1, 10, 15). In both cases it is the prospect of betrayal and trial which occasions the call to watch. That call accents the care with which Jesus told his disciples "all things beforehand," and yet also the somber fact that all of them were nevertheless led astray. This danger of being demoralized by the onset of persecution explains the necessity of alertness (cf. βλέπετε 13:5, 9, 23). Disciples might be certain that such sufferings awaited them, but they could not know in advance when the hour of greatest trial would strike. Lightfoot commented on the way in which the Gethsemane scene carries

[4] Cf. Max Wilson, "The Denial Sequence in Mark 14:26-31, 66-72," in *New Testament Studies* 17 (1971): 430-31.

[5] R. H. Lightfoot, *The Gospel Message of St. Mark,* pp. 48-59.

forward the use of the term *hour* in 13:32. The later scene proved that the son had not in fact known when his hour would come, and when he learned that hour's arrival, he prayed that it might pass from him (14:35, 36). Because he had watched for the hour of maximum temptation he had been able to identify and to accept it. The need for watching derived, as in 13:33-37, both from the knowledge that the final trial was near and from the ignorance of the day and hour. In chap. 13, Jesus had appealed to the disciples to watch; in chaps. 14, 15 their failure to do so was documented. It was the master who had successfully watched who commanded his followers also to watch; his behavior thus became the standard by which their failure was judged. This contrast forms the inner structure of the Gethsemane story.

This inner congruity between the situations envisaged in the Apocalypse and in Gethsemane is reflected in the curious coincidence between the divisions of the night which are carefully specified in both the parable (13:35) and the historical narrative (chap. 14). Lightfoot was quite right in emphasizing these divisions: late evening (14:17), midnight (14:30), cockcrow (14:72), early morning (15:1). Austin Farrer was also fully justified in developing the significance of Lightfoot's discovery.[6] The parable stressed the departure and return of the lord, a stress continued and fulfilled in Gethsemane in the departure and return of the Lord to the same disciples. The parable warned against being found asleep. The story tells of that very sleep, not once, but three times. In fact, the story used the very same words: come (*erchetai*), find (*heuriskei*), sleep (*katheudontas*). The story thus illustrated both positively and negatively the action of sleeping which had been mentioned in 13:36. To sleep is to stop praying because one is not aware of the trial (*peirasmos*). To sleep is to be unable to recognize the onset of trial, or to accept it as the will of the Father. To sleep is to lack the strength for one hour's battle with Satan (14:37). Sleeping takes place whenever eyes are too heavy to discern what is happening,

[6] Austin Farrer, *A Study in St. Mark* (London: Oxford University Press, 1952), pp. 139 ff.

when the spirit is weaker than the flesh. By such definitions of sleep the story of Gethsemane illustrated negatively what was meant by watching, whether in chap. 13:33-37 or in chaps. 14, 15. Conversely, watching was illustrated positively by the picture of Jesus in the Garden. He had been alert to recognize when the hour drew near in the form of betrayal and arrest. Although that hour had plunged him into intense distress (14:33), he had been able to overcome in prayer the powers of death and the devil. Farrer was fully justified in concluding:

> The apocalypse is carried into the passion by means of the exhortation with which XIII concludes. . . . The exhortation appears at first sight to be concerned with watching for the end of all things, but as it proceeds it presses with such urgency upon the listening disciples that it must concern their present state. In some sense the days of antichrist must be upon them.[7]

This correspondence between the apocalyptic parable and the Gethsemane story justifies three comments concerning the parable.

(1) Gethsemane reinforces the distinction between the doorkeepers (implicitly identified with the three, the four, or the twelve) and the other servants. The former had a special task (*thuroros*) in watching for the returning lord. They had charge of the door and were trusted with the keys. What happened in the Garden disclosed the degree to which their responsibility carried with it special dangers. They had a special desire and yen for sleeping. Mark may thus have interpreted the whole Passion Story as having a quite special relevance to the continuing work of the apostles and their successors within the church, not because of superior status but because the other slaves (*douloi*) depended upon the faithfulness of these leaders.

(2) If, as we have argued, the appeal of chap. 13 and the story of chaps. 14, 15 were shaped together within the same traditional matrix and thereby came to reflect each other, the decision on the original text of 13:33 may be affected. In that verse many manuscripts include the single command to

[7] *Ibid.*, p. 139.

watch; a much larger number, however, give a double command: watch and pray. Most recent editors have preferred the less well-attested text; they can easily defend that choice. To them the double command appears to be a case of assimilation to 14:38; moreover, the addition of the command to pray seems quite extraneous to this earlier context. But if, in a pre-Markan stage, this parable was shaped as a preparation for Gethsemane, that foreignness evaporates. The assimilation could have taken place during this earlier shaping of this continuous narrative. If so, the later omission of the command to pray can readily be explained as a scribe's excision of something which he mistakenly thought was alien to the parable. In a period and situation in which the act of watching decided the issue between God and Satan, where it was the response of men to a final trial (*peirasmos*) for which their own strength was quite inadequate, watching would have been quite inseparable from praying. A defense can therefore be mounted for the better attested text of 13:33, since the command to pray is no less at home there than in 14:38. In fact, the similarity of the two verses may have been inherent in the oral traditions from a very early stage.

(3) If, as we have argued, there is such extensive continuity in the motifs linking these chapters, we are bound to infer that this long interwoven story had a common history. If the Gethsemane story is pre-Markan, so is the parable of 13:33-37. If one was shaped in oral tradition rather than by a single editor, so was the other.[8] One was not more highly apocalyptic than the other, nor more liturgical, nor more metaphorical, nor more mythological, nor more fully demythologized. This observation undercuts the argument of many scholars to the effect that the command to watch (13:33) presumes the experience of a delay in the Parousia and the subsequent effort on the part of Christian leaders to counter the cooling of apocalyptic enthusiasm.[9] The inapplicability of such an inter-

[8] If the *Sitz im Leben* for one was apostolic preaching or eucharistic celebration, the same would be true for the other.

[9] Cf. E. Grässer, *Das Problem der Parusieverzögerung* (Berlin: Beiheft zur Zeitschrift für die neutestamentliche Wissenschaft, 1957), pp. 86-95.

pretation to the same command in 14:32-33 tends to weaken that argument. In sum, then, there are many features in this longest connected story in the Gospels which mark it as pre-Markan in origin and therefore as coming from the first generation. There are also, of course, many features in its present form which reflect post-resurrection experience. The most decisive influence dating from after Jesus' death was not, however, the unexpected delay in the Parousia, but the memories of the Lord's own struggles with his "hour"; it was those struggles which gave concrete meaning to his command to his servants, whether in 13:33 or in 14:32-33. The command to watch, then, may well have been pre-resurrection in origin, though its content and context in Mark are probably post-resurrection. More important, still, however, than the date of its origin is the applicability of the command to many situations during many years. The very difficulties in dating it are one measure of its continuing relevance to this wide range of situations.

It is worth noting that the references to the Lord's coming (or to the Day of the Lord) visualize it as happening in the night. This may seem strange when it was not the custom for men to travel at night. It is likely that this incongruous element in the parable was therefore occasioned by the symbolic notion of night and by the implications of the command to wake up and to watch. The Gethsemane story makes clear that it was the arrest of Jesus which determined the special Christian definitions of *night* and *hour*.

According to Luke 22:53, this was the *hour* for the demonstration of the authority and power of *darkness*. The sovereignty of Satan was embodied in the violence of the soldiers, elders, and chief priests, making this their *hour*, invoking *night* in a distinctive sense. (Many discussions of the problem of whether the trial could legally be held at night are entirely beside the point, because they mistake the kind of language being used.) The same event became in a different sense Jesus' own hour, which he prayed might pass from him (Mark 14:35) and which he nevertheless recognized and accepted (14:41). His *hour* was defined by trial (Luke 22:40), by distress (Mark 14:33), by mortal grief (14:34). For the hour to pass away was equivalent to the cup being removed (14:36). The advent of the hour was identified by Jesus with the advent of his betrayer and his delivery into the hands of sinners. As a result of his watching and praying, the hour which Jesus had not known in advance became known and accepted. The hour which the disciples did not know would be a comparable trial (*peirasmos*), a comparable battle between spirit and flesh (14:38), a battle which would be won by the powers of darkness or the power of God on that *night* when they would also be betrayed into the hands of sinners. Such betrayal would always take place at night, for it was the onset of trial which made the time night; yet its advent would also mark the advent of the day of the lord when he would judge his servants. Thus the configuration of temporal images (night, day, hour, watching, sleeping) conformed to the syndrome of spiritual warfare initiated by this lord as the vocation of these servants. The meanings of the terms in the context of Gethsemane are continuous with their meanings in the context of the parabolic address in chap. 13, because in Gethsemane he gave the same commands to the same men from the same mountain. The only difference was due to the fact that he now knew that his hour had come, whereas they knew neither his hour nor theirs, and therefore could neither watch nor pray with him. Thus in both chapters his command pointed ahead to the time when they would be called upon to drink their own cup.

The Passion Story in Mark is not content to picture the doorkeeper's sleep in Gethsemane; it adds an example of Peter's "sleeping" in the court of the high priest. Just as the account of drowsiness in Gethsemane was shaped as a fulfillment of Jesus' parable in 13:33-37, so the account of Peter's denial in 14:66-72 was shaped as a fulfillment of Jesus' prophecy in 14:26-31, which in turn appealed to the prophecy of Zechariah.[10] Moreover this denial sequence is quite obviously linked to the watching-sleeping sequence. One link is

[10] Cf. Max Wilson, "The Denial Sequence . . . ," pp. 432-36.

the explicit reference to the nighttime and to the narrower specification of the cockcrow (13:35; 14:30, 37, 72). Another link is the fulfillment of 13:9-10; another is the fact that Peter's self-assurance in 14:29 is located immediately adjacent to the story of his sleep (14:37), where Jesus' dialogue with the trio of leaders also proceeds by way of a dialogue with Peter. Peter's hour of trial against which Jesus warned in 14:38 indeed took place before that dreadful night was over, in the courtyard of the high priest. Thus the whole intricately woven skein of events serves as evidence of the central importance of the parable and as a dramatic explication of what it meant to stay awake or to sleep. Sleep connoted the denial of Jesus under the stress of persecution, on that night during which the day of the Lord dawned; watching connoted the alertness of Jesus under trial, along with the resultant courage and forgiveness of such deacons as Stephen, who, in making the good confession, beheld "the Son of man standing at the right hand of God" (Acts 7:56). Although the parable was given immediately before the Passover meal, the proper interpretation of the parable occurred "on the night in which he was betrayed." That interpretation included everything which happened during that night, from the Supper when it became apparent that the disciples might have to die with him (14:31)[11] through the second crowing of the cock, when their treason was complete. This interpretation is, in fact, more important than the parable itself, and this fact explains why the second person imperatives in 13:33, 35 break through the parabolic form of vs. 34. The whole complex of stories becomes a heavy underlining of the single word *watch* as addressed to all disciples.

1 Thessalonians 5:2-10

For you yourselves know well that the day of the Lord will come like a thief in the night. When people say, "There is peace and

[11] *Ibid.*, p. 433.

security," then sudden destruction will come upon them as travail comes upon a woman with child, and there will be no escape. But you are not in darkness, brethren, for that day to surprise you like a thief. For you are all sons of light and sons of the day; we are not of the night or of darkness. So then let us not sleep, as others do, but let us keep awake and be sober. (*I Thess. 5:2-6.*)

When we move to the context of the command in I Thessalonians, the change in imagery appears at first to be very extensive. Here there is nothing about Jesus' inner struggle, nor about servants waiting for their absentee Lord. Instead three metaphorical situations conjoin to provide a new setting for the command. The reference to the thief suggests by implication that the readers are householders guarding their possessions. Their situation is also compared to that of the pregnant woman awaiting childbirth. Finally, readers are invited to think of themselves as sentinels armed with helmet and shield (vs. 8). These three metaphorical complexes are fused with another, i.e., the two contrary paternities of 5:5. The appeal to alertness and soberness is the only element common to all these analogical notions, none of which is the same as those in Mark 13, 14.

Behind these contrasts in imagery, however, are more important parallels. Paul was fully as aware as Mark of the necessity for all followers of Christ to share his suffering; in fact, he had taught the Thessalonians that suffering would be their lot (3:4; cf. Mark 8:34-35; 10:33-45). He now reminded them that in their suffering they had shared in the passion of the Lord, of the churches in Judea, and of the apostle himself (2:14-16), and had thus become models for believers elsewhere to emulate (1:6, 7). This participation in suffering he viewed as normal for those who were waiting for God's Son from heaven. Their destiny would be determined by their firmness in this stance. If they stayed awake, he would deliver them from the wrath which would otherwise overtake them (1:10; 5:9). This pattern of thought is very similar to that underlying Mark.

Even more clearly continuous is the basic contrast between night and day, between light and darkness, with the corresponding expectation that the Lord would arrive in the night. This event was expected in the near future, in the Epistle as well as in the Gospel; but in both documents it was also seen as something unexpected, sudden, and inexorable. In both cases sleep guaranteed destruction, reversing the intention of God for his servants. Only in the Epistle did the antithesis between sleeping and waking merge with the antithesis between drunkenness and soberness. But this did not alter the sense. Again, only in the Epistle did sleepiness coincide with the complacency of those who say "Peace and security." But such complacency was not alien to the drowsiness of the disciples in Gethsemane. The Epistle contributed to a definition of what watching entails, by identifying the loyal sentinel's armor with faith, love, and hope.

In both documents the primary focus fell on the company of Jesus' followers. It is well to stress this fact, because it discloses the flexibility of the images. In Mark 14, the tragic poignancy of the sleep depends upon the previous efforts of Jesus to prepare these very men for their own time of trial. So in his letter Paul was concerned about the thief who might steal "the treasures" of the "sons of the day" whenever they became self-contained and slack. Only drunken sentinels needed to fear the unexpected and inexorable wrath. In other words, the Christian's responses to successive situations (watching vs. sleeping, soberness vs. drunkenness) disclosed his paternity. For a son of light to become a son of the darkness would guarantee the coming of the thief with wrath and sudden destruction. The function of the images is to articulate the decisive struggles proceeding between the power of God and the powers of darkness within the arena of Christian loyalties. The language loses its integrity and its force the moment readers suppose that Paul was announcing a date on the calendar when the day of the Lord would dawn for both the drunken and the sober. The destiny of the two does not belong within the same timetable. It is not so much the calendar that prompts the necessity of watching as it is the character of the watching which imparts coherence to the day-night imagery. All components of this language are metaphorical. Only so can we explain the compresence of day and night, of sons of light and sons of darkness. According to this mode of thought, obedience to the call for soberness makes all the difference between day and night.

I Thessalonians was written, however, because those first readers had found such language confusing. They had received the teachings about times and seasons (5:1, 2), but had misconstrued them. It is likely that in their confusions they had misread Paul's imperatives in the same way as did later readers. One source of these confusions was surely hermeneutical; that is, the readers did not readily comprehend Paul's subtle use of this traditional analogical language. Failing in that, they were unable to grasp the rationale of the behavior patterns incumbent on them as sons of the day. In this respect they were probably not unlike the doorkeepers in Mark 13, who were caught sleeping. Their understanding of times and seasons, including the time (*kairos*) of trial (*peirasmos*), did not enable them to remain awake, i.e., to perform faithfully the work (*ergon*) which the lord had given to them. Presumably this hermeneutical confusion arose because they did not grasp the interdependence of the images. The day was not, as they supposed, something that could be scheduled in advance, but represented a reality which appeared suddenly in the midst of the darkness to disciples whose behavior left them unprepared. They had not laid aside their habit of viewing night and day as mutually exclusive temporal measurements. Accordingly they did not see that the basic contradiction (that the *day* should appear in the *night*) required assigning new meaning to both terms. Primary to this new meaning was the one-one correlation between man's sleeping (the night) and God's wrath, on the one hand and, on the other, man's watching (the day) and God's salvation. Moreover this basic correlation of antitheses made sense only in trying to articulate the two paternities of 5:5. These two paternities, in turn, made sense only in terms of the total process of decision-making on the part of believers. It was by their actions (inclusive of intention, purpose, loyalty, discernment, choice) that they illustrated the relevance of the analogical configurations. The use of the analogies was designed to reveal the source and significance and outcome of each action. The hermeneutical problem could be solved only by reckoning with this intentionality of the language, and by penetrating to the ontological ground which lay beneath each decision on the part of the readers.

Thus the prime test of comprehension was the extent to which the actions of the Thessalonian congregation demonstrated their faithfulness as sons of the day. In some respects they had failed that test; therefore Paul needed to repeat his injunctions. This made crucial their answer to the question: By what type of behavior does watchfulness become operative? This earliest letter of Paul provides a few helpful clues. (1) The attitude of watchfulness eliminates the tendency to say "Peace and security." That is, though watching may not express a knowledge of day and hour, it does express the expectation of warfare, presumably between God and Satan (cf. Matt. 10:34), in which each soldier must accept the prospect of trials and must learn to live with total insecurity. (This is a plausible inference from 5:3.) (2) This prospect requires of the sentinel the constant wearing of a particular helmet. To lay aside the "hope of salvation" would be an action guaranteeing the victory of darkness. Anyone whose paternity is the day holds firmly to that hope, allowing that very distinctive future to determine his actions. In this respect the future precedes the present for the Christian whenever he is caught by the onset of persecution for his faith.[12] I Thess. 5:8 suggests that in Paul's vocabulary any action stemming from this hope represented watchfulness. (3) The same logic applies to the shield. To live in the darkness as sons of light required employing whatever protection was involved in the shield of faith and love. Here the Thessalonian readers would presumably have been able to supply from memory various definitions of faith and love. Each work of faith thus became a component of alertness. (4) I Thess. 5:11 suggested to the Thessalonians other Pauline

[12] Cf. "The Time of Hope in the New Testament," *Scottish Journal of Theology* 6 (1953): 337-61.

coefficients of watchfulness. Here the communal duties take precedence over the individual ones. A congregation stays awake to the degree in which it engages in mutual exhortation, strengthening, consolation, comfort, and edification. Paulinists will immediately recognize the rich and complex Pauline cargo carried by these terms. (5) Although further deductions from the context become more precarious, it is possible that the whole cluster of exhortations in 5:11-22 should be viewed as further paraphrases of the command to watch (5:6). They clearly explicate the mutual upbuilding of 5:11, a verse which is bound to the previous analogies by "therefore." To the extent that this deduction is accepted, the scholar becomes more impressed by the wide range of definite meanings than by the indefiniteness of the command to watch. To that same extent, the scholar sees that each of these characteristic Christian commands gains breadth and depth when it is seen as one of the ways by which the Christian army articulates its knowledge of times and seasons and its participation in the war between darkness and light. Conversely, the more deeply the exegete penetrates into the source and structure of such actions (e.g., pray without ceasing) the more cogent will he find the analogical language of 5:1-10. That language remains highly variable (watchman, pregnant woman, army sentinel), but the necessity of alertness where day meets night remains constant.

I Peter 5:1-10

Be sober, be watchful. Your adversary the devil prowls around like a roaring lion, seeking some one to devour. Resist him, firm in your faith, knowing that the same experience of suffering is required of your brotherhood throughout the world.

(*I Peter 5:8, 9.*)

There are striking differences between Paul's vocabulary and Peter's. In the latter there is no mention of the day/night antithesis and no use of images of the watchman or birth pangs. Yet behind the vocabulary we discern a similar situation. It is the historical suffering (*pathemata*) of Christ, of the apostle, and of the whole brotherhood (5:1, 9, 10) which provides the occasion for the command to watch. Each instance of suffering is interpreted ontologically or mythologically as an episode in the warfare between God and Satan over the fate of souls. In this warfare the Christian knows the certainty of a time (*kairos*) of humiliation and exaltation (vs. 6), though he does not know when the hour of maximum trial will come. Various attitudes and actions, roughly the equivalents or corollaries of the command to watch, become incumbent on him. Here, as in Paul, soberness and alertness are twins. Here, too, steadfastness grows out of the knowledge that because of God's care his flock can be carefree (cf. Chap. 8 above). It expresses the understanding that exaltation and glory emerge out of voluntary humiliation and suffering (vss. 5, 6), and that God's call entails the experience of strength conveyed mysteriously in weakness (vs. 10). It connotes a vivid awareness of the subtle ways in which the lion attacks the flock, e.g., by way of self-concern, fear for the future, resentment over a painful lot. The devil's attack upon leaders (vss. 2, 3) takes a somewhat different course than when he is subverting laymen (vs. 5*a*), though he can be repulsed by the same humility. The true response to suffering, which in 5:6 is called watching, is spelled out in other terms in 4:12-19, a paragraph which has multiple links to Gethsemane, to the Sermon on the Mount, and to the apocalyptic discourse in Mark 13. As the faith of 5:7 signified a disposition which has been determined by the sufferings of Christ and by the disclourse of God's power and glory in those sufferings, so that same steadfastness in faith (which in vs. 9 is tantamount to the watching of vs. 8) signified a disposition toward one's own suffering which conformed to Christ's victory over the demonic lion, a disposition which dictated the whole ethos and ethic of the brotherhood. One can bc confident that both Epistles (I Thess. and I Peter) give comparable and complementary interpretations of the command to watch, interpretations in which the most constant elements are provided not by verbal coincidences but by situational, theological, and ethical patterns.

There are verbal coincidences, to be sure, and these may be even more significant than we have indicated. Philip Carrington believed that he could isolate a standard catechetical form which he labeled *Vigilate.*[13] Following his lead, E. G. Selwyn identified a longer and more complex form which he labeled P for persecution.[14] I feel that the evidence is too varied and too fluid to enable us to recover the contents of such a form. I agree, however, that during at least the first generation, every teacher and every congregation faced the prospect of suffering comparable to that of Christ, that this *Sitz-im-Leben* evoked a basic set of mythological analogies to articulate the conflict of hidden forces which disciples experienced, and that the command to watch, along with its various cognate imperatives, became one of the standard and normative elements in the catechism. This command was focused sharply enough to warn believers of their own most immediate temptation and yet inclusive enough to cover virtually every religious and moral duty attendant upon life within the Christian brotherhood. Because the trial (*peirasmos*) could take so many forms, the demand for watchfulness became all the more appropriate. Thus the interpretation of the dominical command in I Thessalonians and I Peter offers modern exegetes valid and valuable aid in the study of Mark 13 and 14.

We have now looked with some care at four literary contexts in which this demand appears, contexts in which many historical situations are reflected and where consequently the action of watching takes multiple forms. There are, of course, other occasions in the New Testament where this command is voiced, but they provide little more than additional instances of the kind of behavior we have examined. A very brief survey will therefore be sufficient.

[13] Philip Carrington, *Primitive Christian Catechism* (London: Cambridge University Press, 1940) , Chap. 4.

[14] E. G. Selwyn, *The First Epistle of Peter* (New York: The Macmillan Company, 1947) , pp. 439-40.

In Rom. 13:11, 14 the junction between night and day is marked by two antithetical sets of armor; these in turn coincide with various types of work. The discernment of night is identified with the discernment of the works of darkness which are specified as reveling and drunkenness (cf. I Thess. 5:7), debauchery and licentiousness, quarreling and jealousy. Sleep and night here become synonymous with the gratification of the flesh's desires and antithetical to the putting on of Jesus Christ. To know the hour is to act in the light of the day which is at hand. Such a passage corroborates our hermeneutical-ethical exegesis of the cognate analogies.

The same can be said of I Cor. 16:13 where alertness is associated with courage, steadfastness, and the determination that every action be done in love. An even more extensive catalog of the unfruitful works of darkness may be found in Eph. 5:3-20. The sleeper's waking coincides with his producing the fruit of light "in all that is good and right and true" (5:9). Such waking is understood to be nothing less than resurrection from the dead; such deeds are nothing less than the light of Christ. It is in obedience to the injunction to watch that believers celebrate the transition from death to life. Apart, therefore, from full recognition of the ethical realities involved here, it is impossible to solve the hermeneutical problems presented by the language.

This same pattern of linguistic/ethical interdependence is reflected in the Apocalypse. Without doing the works appropriate to faith, believers die; remembrance, repentance, and renewed works constitute the action by which they awake, an action which is identical with sharing in the victory of Christ. The call to watch is a summons to move from this death to this life (Rev. 3:1-6). The prophet places the whole of his apparently bizarre apocalyptic imagery at the service of this call. Awake, the Christian keeps his white garments; asleep, he loses them to the invading thief (16:15).[15] Here it is difficult for most readers to use the ethical factor to resolve the hermeneutical riddle, more difficult than in the case of

[15] Cf. Minear, *I Saw a New Earth* (Washington: Corpus Books, 1968), pp. 148-49.

Paul's more obviously demythologizing practice. But this is not because the language of the Apocalypse is more cosmological, but rather because the prophet holds more firmly to the task of clarifying the ontological/cosmic actualities of the two worlds of ethical discernment.

In Luke the clearest synonyms for watching are provided by two passages: 12:32-48 and 21:29-36. In the first of these, the prescribed alertness in waiting for the master takes the form of providing food for his household "at the proper time" (vs. 42) rather than mistreating the other servants and greedily claiming security for oneself (vs. 45). The thief who comes whenever the householder drowses has no power over the man who invests his treasure and his heart in heaven (vs. 33). In the second passage, to watch and to pray enables a person to escape the destruction that befalls all whose hearts are "weighed down with dissipation and drunkenness and cares of this life" (21:34).

Like Luke, Matthew defines the action of watching by the steward's faithfulness in feeding the other members of the Lord's household (Matt. 24:45-46). This image of the deacon probably embraces all the routine duties of the householder. In fact, more clearly than either Mark or Luke, Matthew uses apocalyptic allegories (all the parables from 24:36 to 25:46) to re-enforce this appeal, and by doing this he compels the reader to resolve the hermeneutical riddles by responding to ethical exhortations. The mystery of the imminent judgment is the mystery of how the Son of man rewards or punishes his servants for their treatment of him when he comes in the guise of the least of his brothers. That treatment defined their watchfulness (25:44-46).

Because the context and content of this command are so variable, it is foolish to attempt to prove that any instance originated with Jesus before his death. When one recognizes, however, the close connections between the command and a large number of parables, the likelihood that this whole strand of teaching is post-resurrection in origin shrinks to very small dimensions.

Implications

We have now surveyed the answers provided in the New Testament to the question: What specific attitudes and actions were envisaged in the demand of wakefulness? We have found ample evidence of the metaphorical density of that demand. Its conceptual context is provided by a thoroughly eschatological vision of ultimate reality. It expresses "the eschatologically marked redemptive situation of the believers in the present age. The admonition to keep awake refers to their state of having already obtained the gift of salvation in Jesus Christ, and it means an exhortation to live in freedom from the sleep of the world, awaiting the eschatological consummation and being prepared for its arrival. It is a matter of living with the day of the Lord and the coming of the Son of man constantly at hand." [16]

There is, however, one danger in stressing the eschatological context for the command. It may lead us to view as extrinsic and expendable the nexus between the eschatological context and the ethical substance of the demand, whereas that nexus determines the force of both context and substance. The demand entails a whole range of ethical coefficients; e.g., to watch is to spend all one's resources in the service of others without fear or favor. The eschatological reality (night vs. day, etc.) is corollary to the action evoked by the demand. We must now try to lay bare the intrinsic constituents of the action.

Alertness as a word describes man's response to God's action, a reality which is destroyed or made unintelligible when either actor is absent. God has chosen the future as the mode by which he will have dealings with this community. Watching is the human action by which this God-who-comes creates new life and light within the present situation. It is also a way of recognizing that at every point and in every moment this newly created community faces the actuality of judgment by its Lord. Greater than all other ills which could befall this

[16] E. Lövestam, *Spiritual Wakefulness in the New Testament,* p. 143.

community would be condemnation by its Lord. The terms of its existence are such that failure to watch guarantees immediate unexpected, inexorable, and total loss of its status as heir of the coming Kingdom. The nature of God and of this community is such that the revival of self-love immediately means the coming of God as thief. The dialectic of this betrayal is such that the thief always comes unexpectedly and always in the night. This moment of damnation can be described simultaneously as the sleeping of the disciple, as the victory of Satan, or as the avenging visitation by the Son of man. The character of each moral decision is such as to involve all three inextricably. Conversely, the power of the Son of man which inheres in the command itself provides the disciple with the impulse to obedience, the power which enables the action of faith. The new life which emerges at the point of awaking conveys all the benefits of the dawning day. The event of obedience is a movement from unreality to reality; that emerging reality, the day into which the disciple and/or community awakes, becomes the substantial content of the action of watching, an action which unites within the realm of salvation the sufferings of Christ, of the apostles, and of "the brotherhood throughout the world." It is significant that the central reality in this realm is the Jesus who issues the command. It is he whose Day provides the light for those who stay awake, he who enables his followers to stay awake. Who else then can execute judgment on those who do not watch for his coming with actions which are consonant with his death? (Matt. 24:36-51.)

There is a very extensive theology implicit in watching, since such an action demonstrates the invasive presence of God himself. This intrinsic theology is coextensive with a complex Christology and pneumatology. He who shares in this action is delivered from the coming wrath because he acts in free obedience to the salvation won in Gethsemane and offered to all men. What makes such an action eschatological is the finality of the choice registered by watching or sleeping, since the stakes are death or life. Yet this whole pattern of thinking makes sense only if true of God's creative activity. The toughest problem for the modern student is not that of accepting an obsolete world view, that is, how to make credible an incredible apocalyptic time-scape which may serve as a convincing basis for this command. Rather, the problem is how to obey an impossibly rigorous demand and to discover in such obedience the temporal dynamics of a life lived by reference to those day/night realities which were laid bare by the death and resurrection of Jesus. Ethical response remains the *sine qua non* for resolving the most intractable hermeneutical riddles.

It may help us to understand the early Christian ethic as a whole if we assess the reasons why it is so different from other perspectives in which the command to watch would be alien or absent. There are indeed many such perspectives in which this command would be extraneous. For example, a legalism which enables prohibited actions to be readily defined and avoided would not be hospitable to this command. "Thou shalt not kill" does not elicit the same set of inner pressures as "Thou shalt not be angry." The avoidance of anger requires a different degree and kind of alertness, as does the avoidance of lust or greed or pride or self-assertion. Where the latter type of sin is viewed with deadly seriousness, there will be located a complex pattern of basic assumptions, including the following:

1. a world view in which the will of God provides an absolute norm of behavior;
2. the acceptance of a final inescapable judgment by this norm;
3. a sense of man's life as the scene of unremitting struggle between the black of evil and the white of good;
4. a consciousness of the dangers of deception by an evil which appears in the masks of good;
5. a keen awareness of the interdependence of believers and of their mutual responsibilities;
6. a knowledge that all decisions spring from desires which have their hidden genesis in man's heart, where ultimate issues are settled.

The urgency of the requirement of alertness is a product

of these assumptions; the more prominent these are, the more penetrating this requirement. In dealing with this command, therefore, we are dealing with much more than the expectancy of an apocalyptic crisis, the mechanical calculation of the world's end. We are dealing with all the mysterious junctions between God's importunate purposes and man's ambiguous and deceptive motives. This is perhaps the ultimate reason why the demand to pray has become in the New Testament the twin of the demand to watch, and why this twin imperative became expressed in the petition: "Lead us not into temptation."

10 Take This and Divide It Among Yourselves

Test yourself on humanity. It makes the doubter doubt, the man of faith believe.

Franz Kafka, in Martin Buber,
Two Types of Faith

In several respects the command to watch must be treated in a way quite different from the other commands thus far surveyed: (1) It is more difficult to trace its history back through successive stages in such a way as to establish its origin in pre-resurrection teaching. Jesus may well have included such a command among his injunctions to his followers, but its context in Mark clearly reflects the impact of his death and resurrection. (2) The command, though applicable to a wide range of situations, derives much of its force from its literary context in the Passion Story. It is so central to the farewell address of Jesus and to the Gethsemane struggle that the meaning of this command has been revealed, at least for Mark, in that dramatic occasion. The command derives its basic content from the trial and death of Jesus, in which his faithfulness proclaimed a final judgment on their fears. It is the example of Jesus' watchfulness and the disciples' drowsiness that is definitive. (3) The command can be called parabolic to a degree exceeding that of the other commands. No one set of actions can be objectively labeled as watching, because it refers to the internal orientation of servants of their absent and returning Lord. Its context in numerous parables (stewards, shepherds, soldiers) has left a mark that is retained even when it occures in non-parabolic discourse. (4) This parabolic aspect is not limited to literary function. The act of watching is as integral to that realm in which Jesus was citizen as it is peripheral to the realm in which the Twelve slept. The two actions disclose two opposing universes.

There can be no doubt that to early Christians the event which most clearly disclosed both the convergence and divergence of those two universes, both the conflict between them and the resolution of that conflict, was the event of Jesus' death and resurrection. Similarly we can be sure that for those early believers the dramatic explication of that death-resurrection was conveyed in the Eucharistic celebration and in the Gospel accounts of the Last Supper. In this concluding chapter we will examine Luke's account to see how he arranges the story of the Last Supper in such a way that the authentic meanings of the Passion became embodied in the verbal commands which Jesus spoke at the Supper. The level on which we approach these commands is the level of Lukan intention, but we believe that earlier levels of meaning may become visible during the process.

Luke's Table Talk

Luke was not the only Christian author, of course, to speak of the communal meals of the early church (e.g., Paul and John), but to none did these meals have greater appeal. As Luke visualized the earliest communes, daily worship was followed or accompanied by daily meals together. The story of Pentecost reached its climax in the picture of the disciples breaking bread together. Such celebration was linked directly to the more cerebral activity of sharing in the apostles' teaching (Acts 2:42). The covenantal sharing of food was accompanied by prayers, by rejoicing, by care for the needs of every member. The supper shared by the Risen Lord and his "slow of heart" disciples at Emmaus was narrated in such a way as to suggest the potential power of every common meal:

"Their eyes were opened and they recognized him; and he vanished out of their sight" (24:31).[1]

The artistry with which Luke described each common meal during the ministry of Jesus cannot be appreciated except by careful study. At the first meal, Levi served as host (5:29-39). It was a "great feast," and the stage was large, for in addition to the disciples a large company of tax collectors and a number of Pharisees and scribes were present. The debate between Jesus and his opponents concentrated upon Jesus' practice of eating with sinners. Why eat with them? As a way of calling them to repentance. Why so much festivity? To celebrate the presence of the bridegroom with his wedding guests. As would be true of later meals, the action and the teaching merged in a single message; together they signified that new wine was being put into new wineskins. Table fellowship as interpreted by the table talk constituted the gospel.

At Luke's second table conversation, a Pharisee was host (7:36-50). Again the dining room became a large stage for dramatic action which was again explained by parabolic discourse. The action disclosed both the faith of a sinner and her forgiveness by Jesus. Jesus actually responded to two sinners, one penitent and the other not, one a gracious host and the other not; his response was again the epitome of the gospel as the mediation of God's forgiveness. No command was issued except for the call to repentance and faith; this call was implicit in the action.

The third common meal occurred in a lonely place in response to Jesus' preaching and his welcome to the crowds (9:10-17). Some five thousand men were gathered together. At first Jesus commanded the Twelve, presumably as the hosts, to furnish the food. But when they confessed their powerlessness, the Master used their "five loaves and two fish" to produce an ample supper for the multitude. Here there was little talk, but much action and profound symbolism, the good news enacted.

At the next dinner, with a Pharisee, there was more exten-

[1] In this and succeeding paragraphs I have drawn on my essay "Some Glimpses of Luke's Sacramental Theology," in *Worship* 44 (1970): 322-31.

sive conversation (11:37-52). In spite of the fact that this Pharisee was host to Jesus, the guest launched into a vitriolic attack that ranged over many points at issue: their different practices of washing before meals, different treatments of the prophets, different stewardship of the key of knowledge. It is probably significant that this long résumé of the woes against the Pharisees should have been staged by Luke at the table, for it showed that Jesus did not hesitate to eat even with pious sinners, but was "reckoned with transgressors" of all sorts, thus conveying Luke's understanding of the gospel.

The account of the Sabbath dinner is a better example of Luke's penchant for locating strategic dialogues at table (14: 1-24). This occasion became a parabolic reminder of the truth: "Blessed is he who shall eat bread in the kingdom of God" (14:15). At this meal there were several parabolic actions, arranged to show various options: the healing of a sick man vs. the care for a dumb animal; the seating of guests in the highest vs. the lowest place; the inviting of rich neighbors vs. penniless strangers; the rejection vs. the acceptance of the banquet invitation. Each of the three parables dealt with table fellowship; each of the three was given an explicit connection to the gospel of salvation; each gained a special nuance from being spoken at table. The presence of Jesus in the home of a Pharisee gave to each option both positive and negative exemplification. Nothing revealed more clearly than behavior at table the divine reversal of social norms and men's reaction to that reversal. It was the man who was "a glutton and a drunkard" (7:34) who had the power to heal and to forgive, or to curse and to condemn, those with whom he broke bread. To eat with him was to become vulnerable to divine judgment and to divine grace. Action and speech at table became an index to ultimate destiny, for every component of the good news was illustrated at one of these occasions. This evangelist could think of no better way of describing salvation than the promise that Jesus "will gird himself and have them sit at table, . . . and come and serve them" (12:37). Likewise there could be no more poignant punishment than to be banished by Jesus after giving the lame excuse: "We ate and drank in your presence, and you taught in our streets" (13:26).

The Passover Supper

Having glimpsed these examples of Lukan table talk, we must now look longer at that most decisive table of all, the Passover feast (22:14-38). Of all examples of supper controversies, this is the only one in which Jesus was alone with the Twelve (here clearly called "apostles"), which he planned and at which he served as host. Here he took the initiative in sealing a covenant in wine and bread. In some respects Luke's intention is disclosed when one compares this with other Lukan table talk; in other respects it comes clear when his version is compared with the other Synoptic versions of this meal.

The contrasts with the other Synoptists suggest that Luke made several intentional changes in the earlier versions of the Last Supper. The process of justifying our interpretation is too complex to review here. We may have attributed to Luke changes which were made by an earlier collector. Luke may have had access to a tradition which was very different from Mark. Being fully aware of those possibilities, I have based my deductions on two conclusions which are at least tenable: that the shorter reading of Luke's text (omitting vss. 19*b*-20) is original, and that his major written source was Mark. I believe that the very extensive changes in the Markan text were a result of conscious intentions.

With his introduction in vss. 15, 16, Luke stresses the close bond between the meal and Jesus' death ("before I suffer"), and also between it and the impending celebration in the kingdom of God. The great intensity of Jesus' desire underscores the importance of this occasion as Luke understood it. Alone of the Synoptists, he places first the blessing of the cup. Alone he phrases the command: "Take this, and divide it among yourselves." The taking as well as the drinking was their act; so, too, was the division of the cup in such a way as to include all of them, but not to include Jesus until their reunion in the Kingdom. The greatest change in the story, however, was the inclusion of four separate dialogues, each of which anticipates developments which took place almost immediately. So strongly did Luke accent these dialogues that he abruptly broke off the words of institution in order to describe those dialogues. I would even make so bold as to suggest that those dialogues provide the distinctive Lukan interpretation of the sacramental command: "Take this and divide it among yourselves."

The Dialogues

How does he introduce *the first dialogue* (22:21-23)? By a very rough and probably intentional break after the words "This is my body." All of us who are acquainted with the words of institution want to go on and say something else. But, as if there were a huge dash, there comes a shocking interruption: "But behold [Stop, look! Can this be?] the hand of him who betrays me is with me on the table"—my traitor's hand is here with my hand on the same table.

"And they began to question one another, which of them it was that would do this." This is a familiar dialogue, and we are well acquainted with its sequel in Gethsemane: "While he was still speaking, there came a crowd, and the man called Judas, one of the twelve, was leading them. He drew near to Jesus to kiss him; but Jesus said to him, 'Judas, would you betray the Son of man with a kiss?'" So familiar is this sequel that we seldom notice that in the earlier dialogue none of the disciples had known who would be the traitor. All of them had been uncertain and had begun to dispute with one another which of them might betray him. Jesus saw this treachery as a fulfillment of prophecy: "The Son of man goes as it has been determined; but woe to that man by whom he is betrayed." This betrayal had earlier been interpreted (22:3-6) as the triumph of Satan. Satan had entered into Judas called Iscariot, and he went away and conferred with the chief priests. Thus the final meal of Jesus with the

Twelve marked the apparent triumph of Satan. The cup had been divided among Satan's pawns.

The second controversy (22:24-27) was a dispute over which of them was the greatest. This, like the previous episode, involved all the disciples. In the other Gospels this dispute had appeared in other and earlier contexts, but Luke, with real intent and genius, located the story at this particular point (cf. above, p. 93). Moreover, he adapted the point of the paradigm to this particular setting. "Which is the greater, one who sits at table, or one who serves? Is it not the one who sits at table? But I am among you as one who serves."

Luke's portrait of the Supper revealed transgressors, men who had not yet begun to understand the rule concerning service and greatness. Jesus understood their lack of comprehension, yet he ate with them. More even than this: he served them, knowing that they had not yet begun to understand what service meant. And they divided the blessed cup among themselves.

The sequel of this? When Jesus said, "I am among you as one who serves," obviously he pointed to his death. The saying also referred to this very occasion in which Jesus shared with them the bread and the cup. It also pointed to his promise that they would eat again with him at his table in his Kingdom. In all these situations, whether past or future, he remained the one who served, whose death made him at once the least and the greatest.

In *the third dialogue* (22:31, 32), Jesus was concerned about all twelve disciples, yet this concern was focused on his discussion with Simon Peter. "Simon, Simon, behold, Satan demanded to have you [the plural, i.e., the Twelve], that he might sift you [plural] like wheat, but I have prayed for you [singular] that your faith may not fail; and when you have turned again, strengthen your brethren." The Twelve, Peter; Peter, the Twelve—"strengthen the brethren." Yes, the fate of all was at stake in this dialogue, and the fate of the church as well.

This brief interchange reveals a fascinating behind-the-scenes struggle. Satan also has been petitioning for something. Satan has prayed to God for the right and the opportunity to sift the men. And Satan has been granted his request. God has told him, as he told him at the time of Job's temptation, "All right, go ahead. Use your power to put my servants to the test." But Jesus interposes his prayer that Peter might have a faith that, after sifting, would be restored. Then he would have power to strengthen the whole group of twelve. In the sequel it becomes clear that Jesus' prayer is stronger than Satan's. Satan's prayer is answered. He does have power to sift them in Gethsemane and later on in the trial, but Jesus' prayer proves stronger. The giving of the cup to the disciples signified their inclusion in this battle with Satan and in the powerful intercession of Jesus.

The Fourth Dialogue

The fourth dialogue is the most difficult one (22:35-38); there is great dispute among commentators about this passage. I present a minority judgment. Because this dialogue comes at the end of the sequence, I think it was intended by Luke as a climax to the others.

> He said to them [i.e., to the Twelve], "When I sent you out with no purse or bag or sandals, did you lack anything?" They said, "Nothing." He said to them, "But now, let him who has a purse take it, and likewise a bag. And let him who has no sword sell his mantle and buy one. For I tell you that this scripture must be fulfilled in me, 'And he was reckoned with transgressors'; for what is written about me has its fulfillment." and they said, "Look, Lord, here are two swords." And he said to them, "It is enough."

The pattern of this dialogue is the same as that of the others. All twelve were involved in the encounter with Jesus. They all confessed that they had lacked nothing so long as they had nothing, so long as they had depended totally upon the grace of God through the Holy Spirit. But now, in this crisis, after they had heard from Jesus that imprisonment and death lay ahead, they had already bought two swords. The difficulty here, of course, lies in the command "Let him who has no sword sell his mantle and buy one." It is worth noting that this is not a command which the disciples obeyed. They had already disobeyed the previous command concerning swords and bags and purses and cloaks. The purpose of this command was not to secure obedience, but to reveal the fact that they had already disobeyed his rule. "Here are two swords." Jesus already knew that they had defied his principle. Their secret possession of the swords indicated their transgression. Not only with regard to swords (violence) but with regard to purse and bag and sandals (vs. 35). Like Ananias and Sapphira (Acts 5:1-11), they had violated their communal vows by an action compounded of deceit, greed, and fear. "He was reckoned with transgressors" had its fulfillment in this very scene at the covenant table. Two swords were enough to prove it. The swords become the two witnesses which must be heard, according to Deuteronomy, before men could be judged guilty. "It is enough."

This is the climax of the Supper. But there is an important sequel, for the swords were used almost at once. After Judas had come up to identify Jesus with a kiss, "those who were about him said, 'Lord, shall we strike with the sword?' And one of them struck the slave of the high priest and cut off his right ear. But Jesus said, 'No more of this!' [Satan has asked to have you. He has sifted you. You have become his tools. Thus far, but no further!] And he touched his ear and healed him. Then Jesus said to the chief priests and captains of the temple and elders, . . . 'Have you come out as against a robber, with swords and clubs?' " Thus Jesus rebuked the police, the priests, and the elders because of their reliance upon the sword. He rebuked the disciples as well. "No more of this!" And he healed the ear. What more effective rebuke could be given than this act of canceling out the wound caused by the sword? "This is your hour, and the power of darkness." This is the hour that belongs to you. This is the hour in which Satan as the ruler of darkness can wield his power. That power is demonstrated by the fact that disciples and captors alike have swords. "He was reckoned among the transgressors."[2]

In this radical revision of the earlier accounts of the Passover meal there is no evidence that Luke had any special theological bias against the words of institution in which so many later theological debates have centered. It is probable that he assumed that churches would continue to celebrate the Supper as a mode of communion with their Lord. He wanted the churches in their celebration to be aware of these four dialogues which encapsulated so much of the meaning of the covenant. These dialogues remained highly evocative of the dramatic conflicts between God and Satan which always emerge in "this hour of darkness." The prophecies of Jesus at the table remained valid for all the successors of the Twelve, for these prophecies were not limited to the immediate treason. Although as traitors the Twelve were commanded to divide the wine among themselves, that division also anticipated the day beyond the hour of darkness. "You are those who have continued with me in my trials." To Luke the trials of Peter and the others created a special bond to Jesus; they were in fact Jesus' own trials. Their struggle with Satan did not finally disqualify them, but rather qualified them to "eat and drink at my table in my kingdom." They had quarreled over places of privilege and honor and had been humiliated by Satan. In full view of that very humiliation they were promised thrones from which to judge Israel (22:28-30).

What may be said concerning the authenticity of the commands which Luke located as having been issued during the Passover meal? We must, I think, assign to him major editorial responsibility for his preface to the Supper (22:15, 16), and for his edition of the command with regard to the cup: "Take this, and divide it among yourselves." He was surely the artist who here as elsewhere deftly arranged table talk as the backdrop for the Gospel drama and who chose the Passover table for this climactic set of dialogues. Three dialogues were

[2] For a fuller exposition of this episode, see my article "A Note on Luke 22:36," in *Novum Testamentum* 7 (1964-1965): 128-34.

drawn from the Markan story: one dealing with Judas (vss. 21-23 and their sequel); the next one with Simon Peter (vss. 31-34 and their sequel. Here, however, Luke fused with the Markan tradition his own special account of Jesus' struggle with Satan for Peter's faith). The third dialogue, provoked by the disciples' competition for primacy, was simply transferred to this locale from its Markan position. Elsewhere we have shown that this teaching has developed from a very early nucleus (cf. above, pp. 84 ff.). The promise of thrones was probably drawn from Q, and was also assigned to this locale by Luke as further illustration of the paradox of the forgiveness of these sinners.

Only one pericope in the series was not drawn from the traditions common to the Synoptics: the dialogue in vss. 35-38 which Luke assigned to the climactic place in the series. Yet this is not so ungrounded as it might seem. It is explicitly anchored in the earlier requirement that disciples must sacrifice homes, possessions, and financial security. That requirement had been stressed in both Mark and Q (Mark 6:8-9; Matt. 10:9-15; Luke 9:1-6; 10:1-9); the Passover flashback in 22:35 asserted that as long as they had obeyed that requirement they had lacked nothing. This dialogue was also anchored in the Markan account of the sword-play in Gethsemane (14:47). At most, Luke was accountable here for drawing attention to the contradiction between the earlier unarmed courage and their present armed panic, and for seeing in this contradiction a fulfillment of Isa. 53:12.

In this as in other examples of table talk, Luke matched action with words, using both together as witnesses to the gospel. The basic question of authenticity therefore is whether Jesus' death actually carried these meanings which Luke assigned to it and whether in the Passover celebration those meanings were faithfully expressed. Did that gathering about the table embody those sharp contradictions between the one who served and those who were saved? Were the disciples as disloyal and self-deceived as those dialogues indicated? Did Jesus exercise such merciless judgment on those disloyalties and at the same time issue such gracious promises to the transgressors with whom he chose to be reckoned? Did their obedience to his command "Take this, and divide it among yourselves" involve them inescapably in dilemmas precisely like those described in the Lukan account?

For me these are rhetorical questions, for I think the answers are quite clear. I believe that the actions of Jesus and his disciples on that ancient occasion were such as to give a basic validity to the four dialogues. Those dialogues were entirely in accord with demands which Jesus almost certainly had earlier levied on his followers. They supplement the ways in which the other demands had expressed the onset of God's judgment, the imminence of the new creation, and the character of genuine repentance and faith. Because he was reckoned with transgressors (as staged so vividly in Luke's drama), the division of his cup among them brought the powers of God's Kingdom into their midst. He could save them only by serving them.

Luke's freedom in assigning to the Eucharistic feast commands whose origin had belonged to an earlier date illustrates one important truth. After Jesus' death none of his earlier commands could remain unchanged by that event and by its vindication in the resurrection. That event defined, both positively and negatively, the content of the behavior which he had prescribed. It disclosed the kind of warfare between God and Satan into which he called men. It communicated his authority to issue impossible mandates and incredible promises. It illustrated better than words the kind of future which now awaited obedience, the kind of hope which in a curious way conveyed the mysterious and miraculous power to obey. After this vindication none of his commands could be unaffected by the story of what had happened. Every imperative would now be preceded by a whole series of indicatives: "the time is fulfilled, . . . the Lord is risen indeed, . . . we have peace with God. . . ." Yet these indicatives annulled none of the demands. In fact, disciples were allowed even less room for alibis, since they had now continued in his trials and had drunk the covenantal cup which he offered. Obedience to the Eucharistic invitation became linked forever to obedience to all the other commands. Such obedience was in fact the sign of standing at the boundary between the two worlds of man's actual choices: the one world in which the love commandment is integral, and the other world where that commandment, however much admired and repeated, is abrogated at the first flash of fear or anxiety. Luke's exegesis of the Passover can thus stand as a summary of our effort toward a better understanding of the commands of Christ.